BRITANNIA

ROYAL NAVAL COLLEGE

1905 – 2005

BRITANNIA
ROYAL NAVAL COLLEGE

1905 – 2005

A Century of Officer Training at Dartmouth

Dr Jane Harrold and Dr Richard Porter

PUBLISHER`S ACKNOWLEDGEMENT

Full and grateful acknowledgement is given to the Commodore and staff of the Britannia Royal Naval College and to the Chairman and Trustees of the Britannia Association for their support and involvement in the publication of this book.

First published in the United Kingdom in 2005 by Richard Webb, Publisher

Text copyright © 2005 Dr Jane Harrold and Dr Richard Porter

Illustrations © 2005 Britannia Royal Naval College (unless otherwise credited)

Design and typography © 2005 Richard Webb, Publisher

The right of Dr Jane Harrold and Dr Richard Porter to be identified as the authors of this work have been asserted by them in accordance with the Copyright, Designs and Patents Act, 1988

Edited and indexed by Michael Forder

Designed by Laurence Daeche, Anon Design Co., Christchurch, Dorset

A CIP catalogue record for this book is available from the British Library

ISBN 0-9536361-3–5

Typeset in Bembo 12/14

Printed and bound in China
Phoenix Offset/Hanway Press Ltd

RW.UK Ltd trading as Richard Webb, Publisher

Richard Webb, Publisher
Dartmouth, England

THIS BOOK IS DEDICATED TO THE

MEMORY OF THE OFFICERS, CADETS AND STAFF OF

BRITANNIA ROYAL NAVAL COLLEGE

WHO GAVE THEIR LIVES IN THE

SERVICE OF THEIR COUNTRY.

FOREWORD

BUCKINGHAM PALACE.

It hardly needs to be said that the training of young officers for the services is absolutely crucial to their effectiveness. For years, if not centuries, the Navy relied on an 'apprenticeship' system where the young learn by precept and example from their seniors. Considering the quality of leaders produced by this system in the struggles against Spain and France over three centuries, it must have been successful. However, the art and technology of sail and the primitive weapons of those days made no great intellectual demands on the officers.

Come the age of steam, rifled cannons, improvements in fire control, communications and navigation, the need for some system to prepare young officers to cope with these developments became vital. The Britannia Royal Naval College, and its preparatory college at Osborne, were the Navy's answer to the problem. This detailed and fascinating book tells the story of the College and how it evolved to meet the needs of a world-wide fleet at a time of very rapid modernisation and of the challenges of two great wars.

The senior officers, who were responsible for the structure and content of the training system, knew what would be demanded of the young officers when they went to sea, and they devised a system of indoctrination, discipline and instruction that would ensure that young officers joining the fleet would be sufficiently knowledgeable to be useful in an unfamiliar environment.

This book is a worthy memorial to the young men who were trained at Dartmouth and who lost their lives in the service of their country while serving in the Royal Navy.

PREFACE

Admiral Sir Alan West GCB DSC ADC

First Sea Lord and Chief of the Naval Staff

As the United Kingdom marks the 200th anniversary of Admiral Lord Nelson's victory at Trafalgar in 1805, it is also highly symbolic that 100 years later Britannia Royal Naval College's architect, Sir Aston Webb, put the finishing touches to our first Naval College for young naval officers on a hill overlooking the beautiful town of Dartmouth. Both events combine to make 2005 an extremely special year for the Royal Navy and all naval officers, and BRNC's Centenary book is an excellent way in which to mark the College's 100th birthday.

The authors have concentrated on recounting the story of the College, starting with its birth, when it moved from its home in the hulks of HMS *Britannia* and HMS *Hindostan* on the River Dart, which had been training officers for forty-two years already and produced famous Admirals including Beatty, Jellicoe, Cunningham and Fraser. They then take us through the challenges of both World Wars, the drama of being bombed by six Focke-Wulf aircraft and the excitement of training four generations of Royal Princes to become officers in the Royal Navy. Their story concludes with an account of the latest changes at the College, which have seen the largest reorganisation for fifty years, comprising a simultaneous triple reorganisation of the entry pattern for all cadets, a refocusing of the syllabus on professional studies and the full integration of the academic and military staff.

Over the last century, Britannia Royal Naval College has continued to maintain its timeless focus on producing modern officers who are fit to serve in a modern Navy. Today all officers, of whatever specialisation,

spend some time training at the College, which still aims to create and educate a new generation of leaders who are eager to step forward and accept a challenge, who care about their people and who act and react instinctively as naval officers in the front line at sea. As well as having an intuitive understanding of maritime doctrine, the young officers are expected to appreciate the importance of their role as leaders and the significance of the maritime environment in joint warfare across the whole of defence. They should have open and challenging minds, be prepared to think laterally, have fun, and relish additional responsibility. The number of foreign naval officers who begin their training, or attend the College for advanced training, is indicative of the high regard in which it is held internationally and I am always pleased to meet so many foreign officers during my representational visits abroad who speak so warmly about their time at Dartmouth. The newly created *Britannia Association* will draw even closer together, those whose admiration for the College sits alongside their hopes to maintain contact with all those who have passed out of its gates and pursued their own different careers in the Service and in civilian life thereafter. Although the past two years have seen enormous change, it is clear that the College has continually evolved over the last one hundred years, and must continue to do so in order to keep pace with changes in society and the needs of the Service; and not least to ensure that it continues to deserve the tribute paid to the College 70 years ago by Admiral of the Fleet Lord Chatfield:

'If the naval officer ever fails, it will not be the fault of Dartmouth.'

Introduction

The story of officer training and education in the Royal Navy is the story of Britain over the past century. One hundred years ago Britain was apparently at the height of her power. The Empire was at its full extent and its people confident that Britannia would continue to rule the waves well into the next century. However, beneath the veneer of Imperial power and prosperity the seeds of Britain's decline were already sown. Other empires and economies were beginning to grow and looked jealously towards Britain. In order to keep these new, aspiring powers at bay Britain would once again have to turn to the Royal Navy to provide her security. In two world wars the Navy managed to ensure that Britain was able to survive until victory, but by the second of these conflicts Britain's power was all but exhausted. Nevertheless, despite being overtaken by the two new superpowers of the Cold War, Britain and the Royal Navy continued to function as an essential bulwark against communism and totalitarianism. Since the end of that conflict the Royal Navy has once again emerged as an important tool of national interests. Throughout this period of change in Britain's fortunes, coupled with the massive technological changes that have taken place over the last century, so the means and methods of preparing young men and women to be the future officers of the Royal Navy have also evolved. This is the story of that process.

The town of Dartmouth has been associated with initial officer training for over 140 years, since the old *Britannia* sailed into the Dart on 30th September 1863. The early period of training on the river in *Britannia* was recorded in a book by Commander E P Statham, published in 1904; this remains one of the most important records of those early years and as such has been widely drawn from in subsequent histories. It was to be almost fifty years before E A Hughes, Second Master on the academic staff, published the first history of the College ashore in 1950. This was followed in 1966 by Captain S W C Pack's account of *Britannia at Dartmouth*. As onetime Deputy Director of the Naval Education Service at the

Admiralty he was well placed to chronicle the momentous changes that took place in the mid-twentieth century, when the College changed from being a naval public school to a college of initial officer training. For the College's seventy-fifth anniversary in 1980 two of the academic staff, Eric Grove and Evan Davies published a history of the college, entitled *The Royal Naval College Dartmouth, Seventy-five Years in Pictures*. Since 1980 awareness has grown within the Navy of the importance of its own heritage. The expansion of the archive and the opening of the Britannia Museum in 1999 have reflected this at the College. Subsequently more material has become available through donations of photographs and historical material to the College. In addition the thirty-year rule has meant that much more official material has become available from the Public Record Office that was not accessible to the authors of previous studies. As the College celebrates its centenary year it is therefore timely for a completely new and definitive history of officer training at Dartmouth.

Inevitably any such history, while primarily concentrating on the last one hundred years and the shore based college, would be incomplete without reference to the old ships HMS *Britannia* and *Hindostan* moored in the river or indeed to the history of training that preceded the ships location at Dartmouth. It is the history of Royal Naval officer training prior to Dartmouth that is introduced in the first chapter before a description of life on the old ships and an examination of training at that time. By the end of the nineteenth century, however, it was becoming clear that if Britain was to maintain her position the Royal Navy would have to reform. This would require not only technological advances in ships and armaments but also a radical reworking of the way in which the Navy trained and educated its officers of the future. The old hulks were clearly no longer the appropriate venue for teaching the naval officers of the twentieth century. Consequently in 1898 the foundations were laid for a modern, shore-based College.

With the inspiration of royal architect Sir Aston Webb the new college was clearly built to impress, in bricks and mortar, that the Royal Navy remained confident in its task, as carved in stone on the front of the building, to promote Britain's 'wealth, prosperity and peace.' The second chapter of the book therefore examines the building itself and how it relates as a piece of classic Edwardian architecture.

Naval education and training is critically examined in two chapters, the first covering the early years up to 1945 and the importance of the Selborne-Fisher Scheme. This new scheme of naval education, introduced by First Lord of the Admiralty Lord Selborne, and inspired by Second Sea Lord Admiral Fisher, was revolutionary by the standards of the day, emphasising the importance of practical engineering, science, history and modern languages. It aimed to provide the Navy with a common entry of twelve to thirteen year old boys for all executive, engineer and marine officers. In particular it was an attempt to break the traditional barriers, largely class based, between the executive and engineering branches, which was becoming increasingly anachronistic as the engine room became the heart of the modern warship. Although the Selborne scheme was to fail both to encompass Royal Marine officers and remove the stigma of the engineering branch it was, in modified form, to provide basis for the most common route for officers joining the Royal Navy until after the Second World War.

A further chapter of education focuses on the major changes introduced after the Second World War, and an era of almost continuous change that has permeated BRNC's second half century. With a new Socialist government in power the apparently elitist system of entry at thirteen, which was seen to benefit public school boys for whom thirteen was the natural age of progression from preparatory to senior school, was ceased. A new scheme was introduced based upon a sixteen-year-old entry and all fees were abolished. However, before this system had even produced its first Lieutenant for the fleet it was judged to be failing and a further review was initiated. The findings of this review actually found in favour of a return to the thirteen-year-old entry, but this was clearly unfeasible in the political climate of the time. Instead it was decided to turn to an all eighteen-year-old entry. Eighteen year olds had been entering the Navy since the Special Entry scheme was introduced by Winston Churchill in 1913 but the introduction of an all eighteen entry in 1955 was to lead to a complete transformation of the College. No longer was Dartmouth a public school, with a headmaster, masters and schoolboys, but a tertiary college, with a director of studies, lecturers and students of university age.

Both World Wars had a dramatic effect on the College, the first conflict seeing early mobilisation of the whole of College. On August 1st 1914 the Captain received a telegram from Plymouth ordering the immediate mobilisation of the College. Before the day was out all the ship's company and all the cadets, some just fifteen years old, were sent off to their billets in Plymouth, Portsmouth and Chatham. Amongst those boys sent away from the College that day were thirteen cadets who were to be among the fatalities on board HMS *Cressy, Aboukir* and *Hogue* in September 1914. Throughout the rest of the Great War, the College's student population was to fluctuate according to the manning requirements of the fleet. A national debate had surrounded the issue of cadets at sea during wartime, the Admiralty finally conceding to reimburse the parents of midshipmen killed in action, a proportion of their annual fees.

The outbreak of the Second World War in September 1939 failed to break the daily routine to the same extent as the First. However, in September 1942 the war came to Dartmouth when six Focke-Wulf aircraft dropped their payload over the College, two bombs hitting their target in opposite corners of the quarterdeck. Fortunately, the attack had taken place one week before the start of term, consequently casualties were light although there was one fatality. Nevertheless, the damage sustained had rendered the building unfit for its intended task, requiring the College – students and staff – to seek refuge at Eaton Hall in Cheshire, where the Royal Naval College remained until repairs at Dartmouth were complete in September 1946. Meanwhile the College buildings themselves were put to use as a base first for Combined Operations and later by the United States Navy, as a training establishment in the run up to the D-Day landings in June 1944.

The College has had a long connection with the Royal family, dating back to the 1870s, when the Prince of Wales decided to send his two sons, Albert Victor and George, to be educated at Dartmouth on board *Britannia*. George V was to send his own three sons, Edward, Albert and George to Dartmouth, between 1909 and 1920. In 1939, Prince Philip of Greece joined the Special Entry at Dartmouth, when legend would speculate that he and the future Queen first met. More recently both Prince Charles and Prince Andrew have passed through the College.

Although this is generally a historical survey commemorating the College's centenary, the College continues to deliver the same core aims and objectives that it has always done. Despite the many changes, not only to the College but also to the Royal Navy and indeed the nation, its mission remains the same: to train and educate naval officers for the demanding challenges of the front line. The book therefore concludes with a look at College life in the twenty-first century and its vision for the future.

Dr Jane Harrold
Dr Richard Porter
Dartmouth 2004

An oil painting (artist unknown) showing HMS Britannia *and HMS* Trafalgar *at Portland circa 1862. Also depicted are cadets boarding the steam paddle tender ready to go ashore.*

as 'gangway paper' and it was still possible to order such 'gangway paper' from the HM Stationery Office as late as the 1950s. Although the *Britannia* arrived at Dartmouth fully rigged, she was to lose her main and mizzen masts in the years to follow, to allow space for structures to be erected on the upper deck, as a watercolour of her in the college collection, painted in 1868 by John Mogford, testifies.

There were two major innovations introduced in the latter half of the 1860s, once life aboard the *Britannia* and *Hindostan* had settled into some sort of routine. The first of these was the arrival at Dartmouth of HMS *Bristol*, a steam frigate that had been recommissioned as a sea–going training ship for cadets. They would spend a year in her after leaving the *Britannia*. In the 1980s a more modern HMS *Bristol* would again take cadets to sea as part of the Dartmouth Training Squadron. The second innovation was the proposal in 1869 of a competitive entrance examination, the introduction of which was accompanied by an increase in the time spent under training and a reduction in the number of cadets entering the ship. Since the increase in the intake of 1864 there had been a steady decline in the entry, the number having fallen to 121 by the end of the decade. The age of entry at this time was between twelve and thirteen years of age.

Britannia was now showing her age and there were signs of decay, but in spite of a smaller number on board more modern approaches to education demanded modern accommodation, and additional study areas were required. These factors led to *Britannia* being condemned as too small for what was then required of her and to her subsequent replacement. Her figurehead was removed and given pride of place on the bows of the new *Britannia*, where she remained until the old ship was broken up in 1916. The figurehead then found a home in Sandquay Woods, close to the racquet courts, before being moved to a prominent position in front of the main mast of the college, from here she was moved to the parade ground sometime in the 1920s or 1930s. Here she remains to this day, but not in her original state, for by the early 1990s she was suffering from the effects of 170 years of being exposed to the elements and the original timber had rotted beyond repair or restoration. The figurehead was transported to Nottingham where a full size resin replica was made and then returned to Dartmouth to take pride of place once more on the parade ground. Other relics of the first (1820) *Britannia* survive; these being two of the four transom figures that held up the stern gallery of the old ship. All four had been removed and brought ashore, two were located in the gymnasium at Sandquay and the other two guarded the path up to the playing fields, where they still stand to this day.

Above: The first of the Britannias *to serve as the Royal Naval College, moored in the River Dart in the condition in which she arrived circa 1863.*

Above right: HMS Britannia *and* Hindostan *moored off Sandquay.*

Right: 'Dress ship' for the King's birthday on HMS Britannia.

Britannia at Dartmouth 1869 – 1905

A much larger vessel that had been specifically adapted for the task replaced the old *Britannia* in 1869. She arrived in the Dart with only a foremast, so that her handsome hull unfortunately showed her off as a hulk from the very outset. She had been laid down as a sailing three-decker warship in 1848 but altered and lengthened during building into a screw ship that was launched as the 131 gun *Prince of Wales* in 1860. Since her launch she had been laid up at Portsmouth, a not uncommon practice in the mid nineteenth century, when ships took a long time to build, but a relatively short time to mast, rig and fit out, hence they were often built in peace time and laid up until

needed. Since her launch she had been superseded by the new ironclads that had rendered ships of her type obsolete. Surplus to operational requirements, therefore, she had her engines and boilers removed until receiving a new lease of life when fitted out for her new task, renamed HMS *Britannia* and despatched to Dartmouth.

In April 1875 the first civilian instructor was appointed to *Britannia*. The Rev. J C P Aldous, a Dartmouth resident with a family and house ashore, was appointed as the Chief Naval Instructor, causing some concern both with naval instructors on board *Britannia* and further afield. The Admiralty had decided to go outside the service for the appointment of this young man, who was to have much older and more experienced naval instructors under his authority. The Rice Committee enquiry that was conducted the previous year had looked at the health and general training of cadets and it may have been one of their recommendations to seek new blood outside the service. Although the health of the cadets was initially of concern, the committee visited the Royal Naval School at New Cross, the Greenwich Hospital School and Eton College and after comparing the physique of the cadets with similar aged boys from these institutions, came to the conclusion that they were larger and fitter, the opinion being reached that life aboard *Britannia* was good for them. The committee did however suggest a number of recommendations regarding the training and in particular the length of time spent on certain subjects. The building of a college ashore was considered at this stage but not acted upon.

It may be appropriate at this point to consider the health provision on *Britannia* and *Hindostan*. Both the Rice Committee (1875) and the Wellesley Committee (1876) reported upon the conditions prevailing on the two ships and the health of the cadets. The Admiralty Papers, housed in the Public Record Office for the period, show that there were a number of cases of illness on board, particularly in the winter, many of which were the sort of childhood infectious disease associated with schools. The sickbay on board in 1875 appears to have been very busy with cases of dysentery in January, croup and whooping cough in March and April, measles in June and chicken pox, scarlet fever and scarlatina in December. The last two, which began in the town, led to the cadets breaking up early and being sent home, as the ship could not cope with the problem. The following year there were cases recorded of diphtheria in January, followed by measles, which kept recurring between March and July, and scarlet fever was to return to Dartmouth again in 1877. Measures were taken to prevent contagion, presumably successfully since there is no subsequent record of cadets contacting the disease.

Contagion was the major concern with all the cadets living in close proximity to each other. Sick cadets were quickly moved off the ship to the cadet hospital ashore, or sent home if they were fit to travel. Measles and whooping cough cases were often sent home, particularly in March near to the end of term. There was one recorded case of dysentery when the cadet was kept on board for four days and the case for this had to be made very forcefully. In August 1877 the sick quarters ashore were inspected by the Medical Director General to ensure that no epidemic or infectious diseases had occurred, he concluded that none had.

The original cadet hospital was 'Ford House', a large former residence set in its own grounds at Townstal. However the cadet hospital referred to above was in Ridgehill from 1871 to 1891,

Watercolour by John Mogford showing Britannia *in the Dart circa 1868.*

Crew and staff members of Britannia *during the 1860s,
Captain Powell and the Reverend Inskip are prominent in the front row.
(Dartmouth Museum).*

The Britannia Museum

*A*s the site of officer training for the Royal Navy for the past century Britannia Royal Naval College in many aspects resembles a living museum, not unlike a stately home, in which modern day-to-day life exists in parallel with a rich history and tradition. This connection was recognized by lecturer and former museum curator Dr Richard Porter. In 1999 Commodore Roy Clare, who went on to become Director of the National Maritime Museum at Greenwich, agreed and enthusiastically supported the establishment of the Britannia Museum. HRH The Duke of Edinburgh KCB opened the Museum on 27th July on the occasion of his diamond jubilee reunion, held at the College.

The museum tells the story of officer training at Dartmouth from the time of the arrival of Britannia in the Dart in 1863 until the present day. The displays include artifacts associated with the history of the College and a number of prestigious works of art. At the centre of the display of life on board the old Britannia is a fully restored cadet's sea chest which would have been supplied in 1911 by Gieves, Matthews and Seagrove of Portsmouth, now Gieves and Hawkes, to a cadet when he joined the Royal Naval College at Osborne. Originally costing £5 10s, beautifully appointed with brass fittings and clips for dirk, telescope and parallel rule. The lift out trays include a 'private till' and a section containing a tooth glass

and soap tray. Mr Robert Gieve presented the sea chest to the College in 1978. The museum also has an example of the later two-tier chest with a drop down front, that was introduced, in the interests of economy, in 1912 and 1913. These remained in use at the college until 1955-6 with the introduction of the eighteen year old entry, when the 'chest flats' were divided into smaller cabins.

The museum also boasts a collection of artefacts made from timber recovered from the old Britannia and these include a fine armchair and two picture frames that hold photographs of the Royal Princes Edward and George, taken in 1877, when they joined the old ship. The dirks that belonged to the two royal cadets, both inscribed with their names,

Bone model of HMS *Britannia* made by Napoleonic French prisoners of war, presented to the College by Lieutenant Commander H. Morton Lee RNVR in 1947.

A standard Naval issue plate made by the Bovey Tracey Pottery Company around 1880, one of the many pieces recovered from the bed of the River Dart. The number shows which mess it belonged to, thus ensuring each mess kept its own crockery.

are also among the prestigious items on display, together with their punishment records from on board HMS Britannia.

The museum also boasts a fine collection of bone ship models made by French prisoners of war that were captured and interned in England during the Napoleonic wars. These craftsmen used the bone from their daily mutton ration, human hair for the rigging and any other material that they could find or trade to produce these intricate models. The bulk of this collection is on loan from Mrs R. A. Wootten and is a part of the late A. J. Cadbury collection. Two of the models are of the late Britannia, the large and particularly fine example being given to the college in 1947 by the Earl of Cork and Orrery. There is also an 'Admiralty Board' model of HMS Royal George. These models were made by the designer to be presented, as a proposal for a new ship, to the 'Admiralty Board' for their approval; if accepted they would then become a working model for the shipwright. Typically they are not planked below the waterline to show the method of construction, but this example is, with just one plank omitted to show the rib structure.

The collection policy of the Museum is directed at items related to the history of the College and all those who have passed through it. One area of active collection being artefacts recovered from the bed of the River Dart where the two hulks were moored. Diving on this site has revealed a large collection of pottery, bottles and other items that give a valuable insight into life on board. Many of these items are on display, some of which are in a remarkably well preserved condition.

The Heritage collection of the College is not only to be found in the museum, but many other items can be seen elsewhere, including the two Victoria Crosses, the Royal Verge and many fine paintings and ship models. Nor does it only include pictures and artefacts; the College Archive (maintained by Dr J. Harrold) is the repository for the 'Defaulters Books' from the old Britannia[1], and many 'Midshipman's Journals'. The Heritage collection also includes the fine historical collection of books of the College library that is much used by researchers of naval history.

Inside the Britannia Museum. Displays include a cadet's sea chest circa 1911, a writing desk and chair from the Royal Yacht *Victoria* and *Albert* and a chair made from timber from the old *Britannia*.

HRH The Prince of Wales studies a display of photographs from the College Archive during his visit to launch the Britannia Association.

HRH The Duke of Edinburgh with Dr Richard Porter, the Curator, opens the Britannia Museum during his reunion visit in July 1999.

1 The Defaulters Books list the cadets that entered the old hulks on the river and their misdemeanours and the punishments given. These leather-bound texts with their delightful copperplate script have provided many a researcher with hours of pleasure and record the amusing antics of the cadets.

Artist's impression by Michael Hill (2004) of HRH The Prince of Wales, later King Edward VII, bringing his two sons, Prince Albert Victor and Prince George aboard HMS Britannia *in 1877.*

though a photograph of the cadets outside the hospital was probably taken outside 'Coombecot' another house that was used, also in Ridgehill. However Collinson (2001) states that the hospital closed and moved to Fairview (now demolished) in February 1896. The discrepancy over the closure date and the reference to two different buildings almost certainly is because two houses ashore were in use, one as the isolation hospital and the other as a convalescent home.

The training ship attracted a great deal of attention in Parliament in 1876/7 regarding bullying and the Admiralty appointed Admiral Willes to investigate the matters raised on board the ship. He concluded that there was not a problem but no doubt it did occur, as it did in all other public schools at the time. As has been stated earlier, a competitive examination was introduced in 1869 for all new prospective entrants, this was abandoned in 1874, on the recommendation of yet another Admiralty committee, only to be re-introduced in a much more rigorous form in 1881. The following year the examination was under the control of the Civil Service Commissioners, and was described in 1887 as being 'an examination of absolutely ferocious severity' by Statham (1904). This examination attracted a great deal of interest from certain

sectors of the public as witnessed by numerous letters and several articles in *The Times* newspaper.

In January 1877 the Prince of Wales' two sons, Prince Edward, known at the time as Prince Albert Victor, and Prince George joined *Britannia*. Except for having their own private accommodation they were treated in the same way as all the other cadets on board. Their time in the ship is described elsewhere in the chapter on the Royal connection with the College.

In January 1878 Lieutenant Guy Mainwaring joined the ship as First Lieutenant. He was responsible for the introduction of two aspects of life at Dartmouth that continue into the College's centenary year. He was first of all responsible for the founding of the Britannia Beagle Pack in 1878[2], and secondly he introduced the custom of taking photographs of each term of cadets as they left the ship. Two photographs were taken of each term, one of the cadet captains and one of the rest of the term, they were framed and kept on board as a record. In the first photograph taken Lt Mainwaring himself is seen seated on the gunwale of one of the gigs with the Cadet Captains. Although all of the terms are represented in the college they are not all passing out photographs, some being term groups and others may have been taken on joining. This tradition continues today with all 'passers out' having their photograph taken as a group which is then hung on the walls of the College. The main corridor was the traditional 'rogues gallery' showing generations of naval officers, and many old cadets delighted in finding their youthful photographs and showing them to their families when they returned to their *alma mater* in later years. It was often said that this gallery of photographs linked the Chapel and Senior Gunroom with 'God at one end and Nelson at the other and generations of naval officers in between'. In the 1990s space along this corridor was running out, so the old Cadet Captains were the first to go, but this was only a temporary measure, then the side corridors were utilized, until in 1999, they were taken down and re-located to the rear of the great hall (quarterdeck). It was all part of a scheme to modernise the main corridor, but the removal of the photographs was seen by many to be a break with one of the many traditions that the old boys held so dearly. There are some gaps along the corridors but a near complete set of photographs from 1878 is held in a series of albums that are still maintained within the College and added to every term.

From September 1883 to August 1886 the captain of *Britannia* was Captain Nathaniel Bowden-Smith, he had also been Commander on board from 1870 to 1872 and in 1914 he printed a book for private circulation, prompted by an impertinent question from a cadet who asked what the Captain did, to which the answer came, 'nothing' and when further asked what the Commander did, replied, 'he helps the Captain.' Entitled *Naval Recollections – by a Retired Flag Officer,* Captain Bowden-Smith describes his time at Dartmouth, offering a unique insight into the training during those times. From his recollections of his time as the Commander he opens with a description of the

2 See section on the Beagles.

Lieutenant Guy Mainwaring in the first group photograph with the cadet captains in 1878.

A class of cadets with the seamanship instruction model.

Commander's responsibilities for discipline, upkeep of the two vessels and the supervision of seamanship instruction. He highlights that the French master had an uphill struggle in teaching his subject to unwilling cadets and the rest of his recollections mirror what has already been written elsewhere in this chapter. 'As regards minor matters, (he recalls), the cadets had been allowed to learn the piano and other instruments out of school hours, and at a slight extra charge to cover the fees of the instructor, but this was stopped by Captain Foley, who thought it effeminate for a boy to play the piano'. His recollections as Captain quoted below give us more detail on life aboard at that time.

'I entered upon my new duties with interest but I found the instruction given to the cadets little changed since I was Commander in 1870-1872. In the so called seamanship instruction too much time was still taken up with masts, square yards and rigging, which were fast becoming obsolete, whereas there were no machine shops for the cadets' instruction nor any vessel with engines of modern construction.[3] On the other hand there was a sailing yacht and plenty of boats for the boys to handle under oars or sail, which was excellent, and the instructors were all zealous in performing their duties. Every cadet, whatever his tastes might be, was compelled to attend the drawing classes, which I thought a mistake; unless a boy had artistic talent, he would drop this later and his time would have

3 This problem would not be addressed properly until Fisher as Second Sea Lord launched his radical new scheme for a modern navy in 1903. It can be argued that although the Royal Navy had advanced technologically, it was still manned at this time by officers and men who were of the age of sail and the instruction of the day reflected this situation.

been wasted, whereas, though all should be compelled to attend the mechanical and chart drawing, I should make the freehand drawing and colouring optional.

The only foreign language taught was French. There are of course difficulties in multiplying the number of language masters, and I entirely concur in thinking French the most useful and interesting: but although I did my best to encourage the boys to learn, or to improve themselves, in this one language, I signally failed and later reported to the Admiralty that the ordinary British boy thought his own language good enough and declined to learn any other.

I of course took great interest in the boys' cricket and other games, but I did not find my berth altogether a bed of roses. In the first place we suffered from the many epidemics to which youths of that age are liable – so much so that on one occasion we had to break up for a few weeks before the end of term. I do not mean to imply that the ships or Dartmouth were unhealthy, but these two old hulks had been there for many years and being moored 'head and stern' in the river, they were subject to great drafts in the winter months, particularly between Christmas and Easter, at which time coughs and colds were very prevalent. Other causes of irritation were complaints from the Admiralty that the boys were not properly fed, which of course were complaints by certain parents passed on to me, and at one time a well known physician in London, who had apparently attended one or two cadets, made such a report to the Admiralty that the First Lord wrote me almost a letter of censure, without any investigation of the matter, whereas not only did I frequently attend in the mess room during the boys' meals, but the officer of the day (one of the Lieutenants) was always present as a duty.'

Much activity on HMS Britannia's *starboard side.*

The meals must have improved because the following description of messing in 1899, by another writer shows that it was then of a very high standard and certainly no cause for complaint.

'The cadets' mess was aft on the lower deck and a very comfortable mess it was, and jolly well we were fed. Breakfast – porridge, huge omelettes and buttered eggs, followed by great plates of ham of tongue – tea, cocoa or coffee, all without limit or stint. Dinner was on the same lavish scale – second helpings, puddings, cheese and fruit, while servants kept passing along with big bathroom jugs filled with drink – cider, beer or ginger beer was on offer, with no limit or restriction. Tea consisted of cold meats in abundance, jams of all sorts and, three times a week Devonshire cream in huge bowls and without limit. To ensure that those who had no cash to spend at the canteen on shore were not allowed to faint from hunger during the afternoon there was a free issue of a ship's bun. On turning out in the early morning before drill there was a good issue of cocoa and a ship's biscuit at 7 o'clock.

Coming from a school where feeding was poor and insufficient and the cooking bad, I found the *Britannia* was a paradise of plenty. At that time I often wished that it was possible to have a lady housekeeper with a staff of women cooks to feed the cadets,

but in later years I have quite changed my mind, when I know of a certainty that at a well known women's college at one of our universities the students are shamefully fed.

The prizes were usually distributed by the Commander-in-Chief at Plymouth or by some other officer or man of distinction and on one occasion the Duke of Edinburgh[4] honoured the establishment by performing this duty.

During these years there was some talk of moving the training establishment from Dartmouth "in consequence of its relaxing climate" but I believed it to be ideal for our naval training school. Shortly before leaving I called at the Admiralty on the Naval Lord who was responsible for all training establishments and asked permission to submit a memorandum on the *Britannia* system, proposing certain alterations to the curriculum, and also for bringing the seamanship instruction up to date, but the Admiral appeared to think that change in the existing system was so unnecessary that no further action was taken.'

At least Bowden-Smith had recognised the shortcomings of the

4 This was Queen Victoria's second son and true to tradition he entered the Royal Navy and made it his career. A large portrait of him hangs in the Britannia Museum.

The beginning of the 1890's saw the question of bullying on the *Britannia* raise its head again with numerous accusations in the columns of *The Times* and the *Western Morning News.* These attacks may have had ulterior motives, other than just highlighting a problem, as many came from notable 'Wykehamists' of the time. The accusations were that cadets were being 'fagged' and particularly the younger ones were being particularly subjected to cruel treatment from older boys trying to extort money from them. It fell upon the Commanding officer at that time Captain N. S. F. Digby to investigate and put a stop to it and he afterwards made the following statement. 'It had, no doubt, been going on for a long time, and, owing to the reticence of youth, it took me a year to get to the bottom of it; but I finally succeeded in getting rid of the principal culprits'.

An insight to life on board *Britannia* and *Hindostan* towards the end of the nineteenth century is described by Fraser and Leyland (1898). This graphic description, represents the first impressions of a young cadet on joining the ship, capturing both the atmosphere of life on board at that time and providing an accurate picture of the layout of the two vessels, as seen through his eyes.

'He receives the impression, afterwards confirmed, that the *Britannia* in this land locked harbour, with wooded hills rising on every hand, lies in a very pleasant place, against which nothing, indeed, can be alleged, save the dampness that inevitably clings to the valley in winter. The old three-decker is moored by chain cables in the middle of the lake-like expanse, and just ahead of her is the *Hindostan*. He sees that a light covered bridge has been thrown from ship to ship, beneath which is a floating swimming bath, heated by steam and used for teaching swimming in winter. Both the ships are housed in over their upper decks, the roofs covering, as he afterwards finds, a fine large space for prize giving functions, concerts and recreation on the poop on the *Britannia*, and a new church on the *Hindostan*. But the larger ship still retains her foremast, bowsprit and whiskers, useful relics of her former state. Somewhat astern of her is seen at anchor, the *Racer*, a screw sloop of 970 tons, used for seamanship and navigation instruction and constant spar and sail drill with the ship under way. The *Racer's* predecessor in this service, the *Wave*, a smaller sloop of 380 tons, now lies abreast of the *Hindostan*. She has had her screw removed, and is devoted to instruction in steam and some sail drill. Just ahead of the larger ship floats a pontoon, carrying the dynamos and accumulators from which electricity is supplied to the whole establishment. The river is seen to be dotted, with skiff, dinghies, yachts and sailing cutters for the use of the cadets.

It is now time to go on board *Britannia*. The entry-port brings the newcomer to the middle deck of the ship, which is clear on the starboard side from the wardroom bulkheads aft, to the bows, and is the place where the cadets muster, and in leisure moments indulge in skylarking or dancing, though often they may be seen snugly ensconced in the gun-ports, engrossed in volumes from

HMS Racer *(tender to* Britannia*) at sea with cadets.*

their library. The cadets spend four terms on board, the two junior terms, described as the '*News*' and the '*Threes*' being berthed in the *Hindostan*, and forbidden by an unwritten law, to wear their caps on the backs of their heads, or to swing their lanyards to which their keys are attached; the two senior terms, known as '*Nines*' and '*Passers-out*' have their hammocks slung in the *Britannia*.

The newcomer, therefore, makes his way across the bridge onto the main deck of the *Hindostan*, where he also finds the starboard side is clear. Let us first descend into the sleeping deck, where the cadet's chests are ranged, and, at an appointed hour in the evening their hammocks are slung. The space is restricted, but each cadet has a 'good clear swinging billet,' and every arrangement is made for his comfort, though there is no pampering on board. At the fore-end of the sleeping deck are two very large baths, which can be heated by steam; and each cadet has his own washing place. This deck and some of the others is painted in a hard white enamel paint, so that it is easily kept dry and clean, the gangways are laid with matting and there are also strips in front of the chests. Cleanliness is the mark of the whole place. In both ships it is absolutely perfect, and even in the hold below the orlop deck, where the ballast, tanks, and store rooms are, everything is perfectly dry, and wholly fresh and sweet. Ascending to the main deck at which we entered, we will go still higher to the upper deck, where are six good sized rooms devoted to the purpose of study, under the poop of the old ship, which was raised and lengthened for the purpose. A few years ago it was the custom to take down the divisions of these studies every Saturday, so that the place might be used for service on the following day, but through the liberality of the Admiralty, and of

End of an era: Britannia *is towed out of the Dart in June 1916.*

many officers and parents of cadets, an airy chapel has been built above the studies, very tastefully decorated, and fitted with an excellent organ. The forecastle of the ship, which is roofed over, is devoted to a workshop, and each deck has been fitted with great care for the accommodation of the first and second term cadets.

Returning now to the *Britannia* where the third and fourth terms are berthed, we may visit the cadet's mess-room, which occupies a large part of the lower deck, and affords accommodation for 300 cadets, who can sit down together without overcrowding. The furniture is plain, but sufficient, and the room is in close communication with the pantries, galleys etc., which are just ahead of it, and separated by a bulkhead from the mess-room and cabins of the ship's company, which are in the forward part of the vessel. Descending a ladder to the orlop deck we reach the 'seamanship room', which is immediately under the mess-room, and is fitted with excellent models of ships, anchor gear, torpedo net booms and everything that is necessary in the training of cadets in these matters. We return now to the middle deck, where are the cadet's library, sick bay and sundry cabins, and ascend to the sleeping deck of the two senior terms, which is arranged exactly as in the *Hindostan*, with one large bathing tank at the forward end. This tank holds about twenty tons of water, which is pumped up fresh every day from the river at high water. After a good splash in the salt water there are fresh-water shower baths to stand under. Here, too are the studies, in the fitting and arrangement of which great care has been expended. Ascending next to the upper deck, we reach the poop and the large covered recreation space which has been alluded to, and in which entertainments are often contrived, the

boys looking forward to them with keen pleasure. From this place there is access to the forecastle, which is the only uncovered part of the deck, where the mast is, about which the boys clamber a good deal at certain times.'

Fraser and Leyland also describe life on board *Britannia* and *Hindostan* in the latter half of the nineteenth century. This too is included here, it may paint a rather 'rosy' picture of life at that time, but it is a contemporary account and other sources from the same period do suggest that it is an accurate portrayal. It makes an interesting comparison with life in the College today.

'As soon as a boy joins *Britannia* he is made to realise that, with his uniform, he has one foot in the Service, and is no longer a mere schoolboy[5]. Then he is quickly inducted into the meaning of the word discipline, and is imbued with a knowledge of what is implied as being 'on' and 'off' duty. The distinction between the two is sharp and rigid. 'On' duty the boy sticks closely to his work, and rare cases of shirking are sternly repressed; 'off' duty, he is encouraged to display his boyish energy and spirit in every healthy form. He learns to look on his superiors as his friends interested in his welfare.'

Before we continue with Fraser and Leyland's description of a cadet's day a short description of the organisation on board may help set the scene.

5 The cadets thought that they were in the navy, regarding their pocket money as naval pay, when in reality it was paid by their parents in the school fees, they were still pupils at a naval public school.

A watercolour from 1884 by L. Neville of HMS Britannia *and* Hindostan. *Note the canvas sheets on the upper deck that were later replaced by a corrugated iron-clad structure.*

'The four terms are divided into two watches, port and starboard, these alternate their duties week by week and are known as 'in study' and 'out of study'. Each term is under the charge of a lieutenant, assisted by chief petty officers (usually chief gunners' mates, under a gunner) under a gunner, who are responsible for discipline to the commander, who in turn is responsible to the captain. Each of these officers will take a term right through the ship.

On board the *Britannia* the bugle 'Cadets turn out' sounds through the ships, winter and summer, except on Sundays, at half past six in the morning. They spring from their hammocks and tumble into the baths. At seven o'clock the bugle sounds the 'fall in' and the cadets are mustered on deck for inspection. They are then sent to their morning presentation or drills, every moment is done 'at the double' and cheerfulness is the order of the day. The boys 'in study' work for an hour at mathematics, but those 'out of study' are engaged in either scripture, history or French preparation, or aloft in the tender or 'pulling boats'. Every morning of the week, weather permitting, and parties go ashore for fencing exercises, physical drill and gymnastics work.

The instructors are from the school at Aldershot to implement the new physical training system, those boys that had been in the ship eighteen months in August 1897, had increased 4.4 inches in height and 3.7 inches in chest measurements, these being considerably higher averages than previously.

'At eight o'clock the 'disperse' is sounded and the boys are dismissed from their studies and recalled from drill for breakfast in the mess-room.[6] The 'assembly' is sounded at ten minutes to nine when the cadets muster and proceed to the covered space on the upper deck, where they fall in and are inspected, as is also the ship's company, then the chaplain reads prayers. The boys then gather their books and are marched by their cadet captains to their appointed studies. The chief Naval Instructor has assistants for special subjects and it may be said that all four terms are engaged in the same work but in stages more or less

6 Breakfast consists of tea, coffee or cocoa, always rolls & butter, porridge twice a week, sometimes, hash or curry, cold meat, bacon or fish, and either bacon and fried eggs or boiled eggs and cold ham on alternate days, and sausages on Thursday.

Britannia *on her final journey, somewhere off the east coast of England.*

advanced. Fourteen hours each week are given up by the first term to algebra and plain trigonometry, theoretical and practical. In the second term time devoted to these is reduced, and practical spherical trigonometry and navigation are added. In the third and fourth terms algebra is dropped, but nautical astronomy assumes an important place. These are the subjects taken by the naval instructors; but there are extra subjects that absorb fourteen hours each week such as French, charts and instruments, drawing, seamanship, steam and Euclid. In the final two terms Euclid is displaced by theoretical spherical trigonometry. There is barely sufficient time for these subjects to be taught properly and it is only the closely–jointed system that makes it possible. Seamanship only receives three hours per week, a situation much regretted. The *Racer*, which usually lies astern of the *Britannia*, is used for practical instruction. She takes cadets out of the harbour to learn manoeuvring under sail and to grapple with the problems of seasickness. After a break of ten minutes at eleven o'clock, the dinner bugle sounds at one o'clock. On four days a week there is soup, always roast beef and mutton, sometimes stewed and corned beef, occasionally lamb or pork, veal and bacon, or meat pies or puddings, with two vegetables, and often two sweets. On Wednesdays and Saturdays, which are half-holidays, buns are served to boys in the field. All the feeding arrangements are under a mess committee, consisting of the commander, paymaster, and chief instructor and the officer of the day attends in the mess room to see that everything is good and palatable. The warning bugle at two o'clock sees the cadets once more hurrying to their studies until half past three when

they are dismissed. They then change into their flannels before tumbling into the boats where they row themselves ashore. The immediate purpose of coming ashore is bathing, where there is good deep water and an excellent place to dive from. The bugle 'sounds in' and all the boys jump in and are reluctant to get out of the water when the 'retire' is sounded. Once dressed they have a number of activities that they can avail themselves of. There are numerous boats, racquet and fives courts, gymnasium and a photographic darkroom, for the boys are encouraged through prizes to become proficient photographers. The boys climb the steep steps to the level grounds above where the playing fields are situated. In the summer cricket is played and football in the winter under both Association and Rugby rules. Sport is taken seriously, as it is in all public schools and two cricket professionals are associated with the cricket ground. There is also lacrosse, hockey, racquets and other games and sports such as beagling, the commander and officers share all the enjoyments of the boys, warmly supported by the captain, who is keenly interested in their occupations. It is in this way that the spirit of good fellowship and friendly rivalry are encouraged, and it is impossible to over estimate the advantage that results. A fine pavilion, with every convenience, is on the field, to which is attached a canteen organised by the ship, where cadets can buy their 'stodge' at moderate prices.

The 'recall' is hoisted at a quarter past six, earlier in winter, and is hauled down half an hour later, when the cadets are on board, in their change of uniform to muster for their tea of bread and butter, cold meat and watercress, and on special

'The End of the Hindostan*' by J. W. Pitcher, 1921.*

occasions jam and clotted cream.[7] Evening preparation for one hour follows where the boys attend lectures or are engaged with their cadet captain in further study. The boys take this 'on duty' time seriously and cases of skylarking are very rare. At half past eight or an hour earlier in winter the cadets gather on the middle deck, where a good band, formed of their servants, discourse music. The cadets enjoy these sessions but it is said that the waltz is not popular with them. After God Save the Queen is played there is a warning bugle, cadets assemble, prayers are said and they retire and turn in at a quarter past nine in the summer and nine o'clock in the winter.'

Such was the life of a cadet, interspersed with examinations and prize giving ceremonies until the day he left *Britannia* to join his first ship, when he proudly displayed the white flashes on his collar that denoted that he was now a fully commissioned officer in the Royal Navy as a Midshipman.

In the spring of 1901 a severe epidemic of influenza swept through the ship, this resulted in several deaths, mostly arising from complications such as pneumonia. The result was again that the ship in general and the Captain in particular came in for some criticism in the letters pages of *The Times,* as one parent highlighted, 'that the sewage from the ship was discharged straight into the River'; one wonders where he expected it to go. On the other hand the father of another cadet, Mr N. C. Dobson, *emeritus* Professor of Surgery, said that after several visits to the ship he was quite convinced that the condition of the ship had nothing to do with the recent outbreak. The Admiralty was sufficiently concerned over the adverse publicity to commission an official report from a hygiene expert by the name of Professor Corfield. He was satisfied with the sanitary conditions on board and praised the cleanliness of the vessel, concluding that the disease got on board in

7 Jam and clotted cream was such a part of life that some years later a benevolent lady left a sum of money to the college for the purposes of providing clotted cream teas for the cadets.

The last commanding officer of the ship, Captain Charles H. Cross RN, in the captain's cabin at the stern of Britannia.

some manner which it is impossible to detect. Another letter to *The Times* attempted to blame the food and the condition of the town of Dartmouth. This prompted the following reply from the town clerk.

'Nothing, in the eyes of some people, can be commended in the poor old Brit, or the place where she is moored. The captains are all incapable, the officers and masters are worse, the position is insanitary, and nothing is right, in short, except the excellent officers, which this dreadful institution turns out! It would not be precisely fulsome if some credit were accorded to the captains and officers for this result, and a small share to the Admiralty for selecting as a rule, the right men for the post'.[8]

The conditions on board and the health of the cadets were again to the fore in the minds of their Lordships of the Admiralty. This may have been a factor in choosing at this time to finally build a college ashore. The fact that the hospital was the first part of the new college to open in September 1902, three years ahead of the main building, does give credence to this view.

Once the new college opened in September 1905, the *Hindostan* was towed away and scrapped some years later in 1920/21 after being in use as a training hulk for engine room artificers at Portsmouth and renamed HMS *Fisgard III*.

The *Britannia* however remained at Dartmouth for another eleven years. The college used her for ship's company[9] accommodation and storage, but she too was to leave Dartmouth in 1916. The ship had been sold in February 1915 to Messers Hughes, Bolckow & Co of Blyth because the copper plating on her hull and the quantities of iron and lead that she contained were needed for the war effort for munitions manufacture. While still in the river, work had begun to dismantle her upper works. Her impending departure caused a public outcry and a fund was started, called the '*Britannia* Fund' to try and secure the option to purchase the hulk for the nation and possibly turn her into an orphanage for servicemen's children. Unfortunately the appeal was unsuccessful and she was finally towed from her mooring after forty-seven years in July 1916. Her final journey was via the English Channel and the east coast of England to her final resting place where she was broken up. It was said that she was so strongly built that explosives had to be used to break her apart. Ironically, much of the salvaged metal was not used for the war effort. However parts of the old *Britannia* do survive. The figurehead that graced her and her predecessor was removed and survived for many years on the parade ground, the figure there today being a full-size resin copy. Her breakers were an entrepreneurial company that offered many artefacts for sale from their yard made from timber from the old *Britannia*, these included, tables and chairs, tea trolleys, cases for clocks, garden benches and flower troughs among the larger items, and picture frames, ink wells and miniature writing desks were offered at more moderate prices. The college is fortunate enough to possess a number of such items in the museum collection.

Thus it was that the old hulks passed into history and their familiar sight moored on the Dart was no more. However their legacy lives on in the 'stone frigate on the hill' and since the early 1990's Sandquay has had a training vessel moored alongside the jetty, appropriately named *Hindostan*. While the ships were in the Dart more than 5,000 cadets were trained on them and it is these officers that were to serve through two world wars that are the real legacy of HMS *Britannia* and *Hindostan*.

8 The Town Clerk produced statistics to defend his town and the reputation of the old ship.
9 The term 'ship's company' here probably refers to the crew other than the officers and cadets, although the term usually refers to the whole complement of the ship.

CHAPTER 2

The Stone Frigate on the Hill:

A Masterpiece of Edwardian Architecture

'Sir Aston Webb's enormous college buildings stretching out along the hill of Townstal, north of Dartmouth. They are of brick and stone in a revised and vamped-up eighteenth century tradition, not successful as an ensemble, because the Edwardian-Palladian motifs are not of sufficient bombast to fit the scale adopted. The tower is not high and broad enough for distant view, and the side cupolas are niggling. The towers at the far ends are too small too — the same mistakes as made by Webb in the Victoria and Albert Museum . . . The sick quarters are friendlier and less pretentious.'

The above description is Nikolaus Pevsner's view of the College as described in *The Buildings of England – Devon*, published in 1952. Strangely, elsewhere in his book he confesses that: 'the only building to express the grandiloquence of the Edwardian period is Aston Webb's Royal Naval College at Dartmouth of 1905-9'. Indeed there are a number of inconsistencies in Pevsner's account. Many Dartmothians would not describe the college site as being in Townstal, the building dates are clearly incorrect and he goes on to describe a marble statue of George V by Hamo Thornycroft (1910) as a bronze bust given by George when he was Prince of Wales in 1908. These inaccuracies apart this German chronicler of the English architectural scene was well respected, having been Professor of History of Art at Birkbeck College of the University of London and Slade Professor of Fine Art at Cambridge, in addition to receiving the Gold Medal of the Royal Institute of British Architects for his services to architecture. One

should not, therefore, allow Pevsner to colour one's view of the College but rather concur with the 1945 guide *How to Become a Naval Officer (Dartmouth)*:

'Dartmouth College is that rare product of modern architecture on the grand scale, in that, on first sighting the building, the visitor feels instinctively that it is neither — A lunatic asylum, A prison, The house of a profiteer.'

Indeed, to many, its magnificent facade is awe-inspiring, projecting an image of British sea power that was unsurpassed a century ago.

The Decision to Build

The decision to build a college onshore dates back to 1875 when concern over the health and general training of the cadets was the subject of a report. A committee chaired by Rear Admiral E. B.

Rice, was appointed and the report recommended that a college should be constructed onshore. In the following year, 1876, another report from a committee under the chairmanship of Admiral G. G. Wellesley examined a number of sites. The findings of this committee were reported in full in the *Dartmouth and Brixham Chronicle* of 2nd March 1877. Dartmouth was not the obvious choice; in fact the committee examined thirty-two sites, including Portsmouth, Gosport, Hayling Island, Southampton Water, the Isle of Wight, Poole, Weymouth, Devonport, Milford Haven and Westward Ho. The criteria chosen, from which a decision would be made were

as follows: general salubrity, supply of water, closeness of a harbour for both boating and bathing, access to the sea, recreation grounds, absence of 'special temptations', general suitability, access by rail and proximity of a naval port. Absence of special temptations is of particular interest, as the old *Britannia* had moved from Haslar Creek in Portsmouth for this very reason. It was not surprising, therefore, that Gosport and Portsmouth were rejected but Poole, one site on the Isle of Wight, Weymouth, Devonport and one site at Milford Haven also fell foul of this ruling. Three sites in Kingswear were also considered: Hoodown, Mouthdown and Green Park.

Above: Aston Webb's original design for the college, circa 1900, showing features never actually constructed.

Right: Letter from the Director of Works at the Admiralty to the Captain of HMS Britannia, *confirming the acceptance of the builder's tender of £220,600 for the construction of the new college.*

Far right: Architect's drawing of interior of chapel, circa 1900.

was originally the chaplain's office, a small chapel dedicated to the memory of Midshipman Bret Ince, who was killed in action in HMS *Prince of Wales* in 1941. Within the war memorial itself is an imposing green bronze sculpture of a west of England cog, copied from the earliest Dartmouth town seal. Such vessels were used by crusaders in the thirteenth century and are also evocative of the ships and small boats that left Dartmouth for Normandy in 1944. On the walls are carved the names of Dartmouth cadets and members of staff who gave their lives in both world wars. In addition these names and more details are recorded in the memorial books, which also include those who have perished in subsequent conflicts.

While the Chapel remains the focus for worship on such occasions as the end of term and Remembrance Sunday, two additional chapels exist within the College. In 1956 the first chaplain of the Church of Scotland and Free Churches was appointed, although he and his successors were to make do with a lecture room (E2), which would be converted for services on a Sunday, until it was finally decided to convert the room into a permanent chapel, St. Giles, in October 1963. In 1969 a bronze Celtic Cross and wrought iron communion rails, designed and made by the men at Sandquay were added and in 1981 the Alice Fawcett Walker[2] Memorial Window was installed, completing the transformation from classroom to chapel.

The first Roman Catholic chaplain did not arrive at BRNC until 1980, when Sir Julian Oswald (later First Sea Lord), himself a Roman Catholic, was Captain. A chapel was created at the back of O block and named St. Philip Howard, after an English martyr from the period of Catholic persecution in England. The first chaplain was Father Couch RN, who was also a monk at the local Benedictine monastery at Buckfast.

It is not just the Chapel, however, that has contributed to the life and well-being of the College. The three chaplains themselves provide invaluable support to students and staff alike through their pastoral care.

i.

ii.

iii.

iv.

v.

1 See Chapter 2 on Architecture.
2 Whose bequest also paid for the painting of the crests on the Senior Gun Room ceiling.

i. The Chapel's millennium doors.
ii. Bronze sculpture of a west of England cog, copied from the earliest Dartmouth town seal, in the war memorial shrine.
iii. The altar frontal of white brocade from the same bolt of cloth as Queen Victoria's wedding dress.
iv. Altar Cross by Sir Ninian Comper.
v. The reredos carved in Bath stone, depicting Christ and six of the disciples.

Building commences with the garden (Parade Ground) retaining walls in place. A rare early photograph.

Lieutenant, who appointed Kelly, of Kelly & Watson Solicitors, and the other by the Chairman of the Quarter sessions last preceding the date of the action, for which position Judge Edge appointed Watson. Watson's account of the business is reproduced below.

'On receiving notice

We met at the Royal Hotel, Plymouth. The Naval and Military authorities, were present with maps and co. They gave their views etc. Having heard all they had to say we retired "now Kelly what is your opinion?" he replied "I am decidedly against making an Order. I do not approve of taking any mans land against his will".

I then said; "I am definitely for making an Order". "Taking into account the great advantages to the West of England and the County as well as the local benefits that must necessarily accrue we must make an Order to take the Land. If the Raleigh Estate show fight let the Govt fight it out," Kelly gave way and we signed an order to take possession.

Next Day
A marine was sent who erected an ash pole in the centre of the Estate.[1]
An action was then brought against us on trespass in the High Court which decided in our favour.
The building of the Naval College commenced forthwith'

Architect Appointed
All that remained was to find a suitable architect to launch this prestigious project. Captain A. W. Moore was Captain of *Britannia* from 1894-97 and when the decision to build was announced he recalled:
'It having been decided to build a college onshore to replace the *Britannia* our excellent drawing master, Mr Spanton, prepared plans of the design, which in our opinion would fulfil the requirements, and I sent it up to the Director of Works at the Admiralty. He declined it and returned it remarking he had his own staff and would not require to avail himself of the services of the *Britannia* drawing master. This was followed by the arrival at Dartmouth of one of his staff, who proceeded to draw up plans which were quite

1 The act of erecting an ash pole was a symbolic act of establishing and taking possession.

Sir Aston Webb portrait by Solomon Joseph Solomon

National Portrait Gallery

Above: The original gatehouse shortly before its demolition prior to the building of a new road in the 1960s (College Way).

Top left: The three isolation wings of the hospital, opened in 1902.

Left: General view of the front of the College and sunken garden in the summer of 1905.

impossible, so I wrote to a friend at Osborne (Osborne House, the residence of Queen Victoria and not the College that was not built until some years later) of what was going on and hoped Queen Victoria would hear. The reply was a telegram commanding me to Osborne. I dined with the Queen and told her about it. The next day the First Lord of the Admiralty was sent for and shortly afterwards Mr Aston Webb was appointed as architect to the new naval college. When Mr Aston Webb came to Dartmouth I showed him Mr Spanton's plans and he was a big enough man to accept them in the main. So the present naval college is to all intents along the lines we worked for. The Easter holidays gave me plenty of time to consider the best site. On one of my walks ashore I went up to the playing fields on the hill which overlooks the harbour. I covered a great deal of ground, but came back to the cricket field with its magnificent outlook. Standing there for a few minutes I was convinced that the site could not be improved upon. I recommended it to their Lordships, and there stands the naval college today[2].'

2 Account taken from the reminiscences of Capt Moore's niece Miss E M Moore. (Pack 1966 p.96)

The appointment of Aston Webb (1849–1930) was not surprising. He was one of the country's most respected architects with some impressive public buildings to his name, most notably the main block of the Victoria and Albert Museum in South Kensington (1899–1909) and the Victoria Law Courts in Birmingham (1885). The commission to design the new university in Birmingham in 1900 rewarded the reputation that he had earned in the city. The early years of the twentieth century were to prove fruitful to Aston Webb, for not only did he have the commissions for two major educational establishments (Birmingham and Dartmouth), he also became President of the Royal Institute of British Architects from 1902-4 and was knighted for his Presidency and services to architecture in 1904. His work at Dartmouth was not to be his last major naval building, for in 1911 he was commissioned to design Admiralty Arch. His reputation for educational buildings was rewarded again when he was offered the commission to design the Royal School of Mines in South Kensington, (1903-13). This latter appointment was hardly surprising as he had the contract to design the Chemistry and Physics building at Imperial College, started in 1898, this was unfortunately destroyed in a fire and now only the tower survives. His appointment by the Admiralty to build the new college at Dartmouth demonstrated the

i.

ii.

iii.

iv.

i. Interior of the Chapel shortly before completion. Note the winged cherub faces carved on the roof cross beams.
ii. Interior of the Quarterdeck shortly after opening. Note the elaborate electroliers.
iii. Interior of the dining hall (Senior Gun Room) shortly before completion.
iv. Bath stone resplendent in the main stair well.

Navy's commitment to the College, in addition its grand appearance would dominate the town's skyline and be a testimony to the fact that, *Britannia* still ruled the waves. The Royal Navy was the most powerful in the world and still had an empire to defend. Such symbolism was important at a time when it was government policy to maintain a navy that could outnumber the next two largest naval powers, particularly, Germany, the United States of America and Japan, with Germany posing the greatest threat to British interests.

The College was being built as architectural trends were changing from the Victorian era of what was often described as an 'aggressive and assertive Gothic Revival' period to a more relaxed and eclectic scene. One aspect of the Edwardian architectural scene was the coming together of artists and architects. Architects now wished to be associated with artists, and through the Arts and Crafts movement they often included the work of artists in their buildings. One of the aims of the movement was to break down the barriers that kept art compartmentalised; architects now started to commission artists to execute carved friezes and sculptures, both features of the new college at Dartmouth. The Art Workers' Guild[3] was formed at this time and the fruits of their labours also appeared on the interior of buildings. Aston Webb was responsible for overseeing much of the ornate interior decoration and artwork at the College and when the Bromsgrove Guild[4] became a company in 1901 he had no hesitation in using the Guild for some of the fittings in the college. The Guild's handiwork can still be seen in the Senior Gunroom light fittings (electroliers) and the ornate main doorknocker, which were both specially designed for the College.

Appointment of the Builders

Tenders were invited for the building of the new college, and the well-established firm of Higgs and Hill were successful with their submission for £220,600 and an estimate of three and a half years to finish the works. The Director of Works at the Admiralty accepted the estimate in a letter dated 18th April 1900. The builders Higgs and Hill had been formed in 1874, from two smaller concerns, that of William Matthews Hill (founded in 1850) and William Higgs (founded in 1867), and by 1900 had gained a good reputation, but the college at Dartmouth was the biggest contract that they had ever won. The company's recent completion of the Tate Gallery in London in 1897 had certainly enhanced their reputation and must have impressed the Director of Works that the builders were capable of such a large undertaking as the new College.

The builders decided that all the joinery and stonework would be carried out at their own works in London. Portland and Bath stone was taken to the company's works in Vauxhall and each week a boat left the Free Trade Wharf on the Thames, with dressed stone, for Dartmouth. The company sent Mr Edmond Hill (Company Secretary and grandson of William Hill) to be resident director of works in Dartmouth, an act that demonstrated the company's commitment to the project.

Laying of The Foundation Stone

Although work on the site had started in 1898, the Foundation Stone for the main building was not laid until 1902 when on 2nd March King Edward VII accompanied by Queen Alexandra, travelled to Devon by the Royal Train for the stone laying ceremony. They boarded

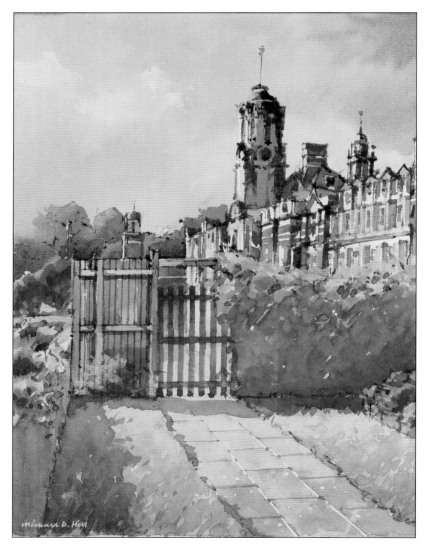

Watercolour by Michael Hill showing the College from the Commodore's garden.

3 Formed along with the Arts and Crafts Exhibition Society in the 1880s to give direction to the Arts and Crafts movement.

4 The Bromsgrove Guild, which became a company in 1901, produced decorative plasterwork, wrought iron and carving.

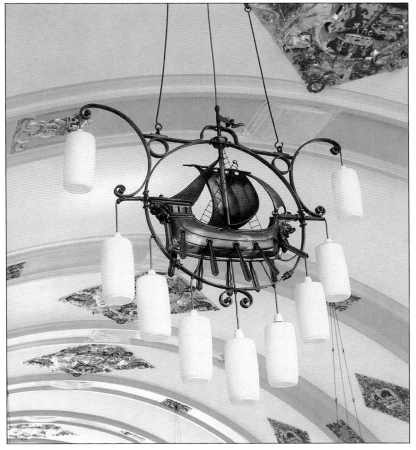

the train at Paddington, for what would be one of the longest non-stop runs that the Great Western Railway had ever attempted. Not only was this the longest run, but the first non-stop train from Paddington to Kingswear. The King took a great personal interest in the running of the train and the railway had chosen one of their best footplate staff, Driver Burden, for the journey. With Burden in charge and the King's interest in the journey, there were no inhibitions regarding speed and the train was allowed to run somewhat ahead of time, reaching Kingswear at 14.55, more than twenty minutes ahead of schedule. The train had maintained a steady average of 60 mph on the open stretches of the line, and recorded an average of 56 mph between Paddington and Exeter, a remarkable feat for 1902. The locomotive hauling the train had been re-named *Britannia* for the day, special nameplates had been made at the GWR's Swindon works, and, as a mark of respect for the Royal Navy, the gleaming brass letters had their sides painted red, as this was the tradition with nameplates on Royal Naval ships. Although Kingswear and Dartmouth had been preparing for this visit for some months, the early arrival of the train must have caused some consternation amongst the waiting dignitaries. The royal party crossed the river in a refurbished paddle steamer called the *Dolphin*. They were met by the Mayor, the Corporation and the Commissioners of the Dart Harbour before leaving by landau for the college site.

A temporary wooden pavilion had been erected over the stone to give protection from the weather should it prove inclement. This measured one hundred and twenty feet by thirty-six feet, there was a raised dais around the stone with seating for the royal party and dignitaries and tiered seating at either end. The walls were covered with red and white drapes and flags, and behind the stone were floral displays and plans and drawings of the new college. The stone was laid in place by a chain and wire rope mechanism operated from outside the pavilion, with orders being communicated by a voice pipe. The inscription on the stone originally had a gilded background, which has unfortunately not survived.

At the stone laying ceremony a casket was laid in the foundation stone. The *Dartmouth Chronicle* described the casket as being of solid silver, richly gilded and enamelled and medallioned on each side, with images of Dartmouth Castle on one side and Kingswear Castle on the other, and containing an illuminated loyal address. The King is said to have locked the casket with a solid gold key, which he took with him. There is, however, a second description of a casket in an edition of *The Sphere* for March 15th 1902. *The Sphere's* description is as follows.

'The casket … measures about 16 inches long by 10 inches wide. It is formed of oak taken from the old *Britannia* training ship and is partly encased in a framing of copper fretted in an appropriate design to show the oak body beneath, the metalwork at the ends being beaten into fixed handles of conventional design to take the ribbons by which the casket will be lifted into the aperture of the foundation stone. The oak lid has a wide framing of copper held by rivets of the same metal and the royal initials 'E. R. VII.' with the

Top: Aston Webb's design for the electroliers in the Chapel and dining hall (Senior Gun Room).

Bottom: Electrolier in the Senior Gun Room today, with an additional two lampshades.

Mess Silver

Military silver has a long tradition in the armed services where its significance lies not merely as a piece of beautifully crafted precious metalwork, but in the story recalled by the inscription upon it, as Roger Perkins describes it (1999) 'This is silver with a human face'. The inventory of silver artefacts owned by the Royal Navy numbers some eight thousand items, many of these given to Wardrooms by 'The Leavers'[1]. In contrast the relatively small Corps of seven thousand officers and men of The Royal Marines boast four thousand such items on their inventory of silver, and this does not include items given directly to the Messes of individual units.

Statue of Britannia:
A table centrepiece given by seven officers in 1896. It was made by a London silversmith from drawings made by J. Humphrey Spanton who was the senior drawing master on *Britannia* from 1867 to 1904. This item is still in regular use as the centrepiece for the top table in both the Wardroom dining room and the Senior Gunroom.

Statue of Britannia with the Prince of Wales Feathers:
This silver centrepiece of Britannia with the Prince of Wales plume of three ostrich feathers rising from the helmet was presented to the College by the Prince of Wales to commemorate his initial Naval Training at the College from September to October 1971. The statue stands on a mahogany pedestal, reputed to be made from the boss of an aircraft propeller; the Prince of Wales trained as an aviator.

The Beagle Trophy:
Made in 1898 with a London hallmark, the BB standing for the Britannia Beagles. Although this is a handsome piece of silver it is more interesting for its provenance. It was given by Commander C. Cradock to the 'Wardroom Officers'. He later became Rear Admiral Sir Christopher Cradock KCVO CB, and commanded the British squadron at the Battle of Coronel, where on 1st November 1914, he went down with HMS *Good Hope*.

Cigarette Box:
A casket pattern cigarette box with a fine enamelled coloured image of HMS *Britannia* and *Hindostan* on the lid. Made in London in 1896 it is inscribed 'Presented to the Officers of the Wardroom HMS *Britannia* by D. Potts Chatto, July 1896.'

The Hamilton Cup:
This cup was commissioned by Admiral Nelson and was a favourite piece of Lady Emma Hamilton. After Nelson's death Lady Hamilton took the cup as a keepsake, but when she fell upon hard times the government of the day took it in lieu of debt. It was later presented to the College.

Alms Dish:
Silver alms dish presented to the College in 1963 by the Mayor, Aldermen and Burgesses of the Borough of Clifton Dartmouth Hardness in commemoration of one hundred years of Naval Officer Training inaugurated at Dartmouth in HMS *Britannia*, 30th September 1863. The emblems within the gilt roundels on the rim are of the four Evangelists.

Plate from Nelson's Dinner Service:
In 1919, twenty-three dinner plates formerly belonging to Admiral Nelson were presented to the Royal Navy by the Navy League to honour the services of the Royal Navy in the Great War. The plates were divided amongst various ships and the College received that of HMS *Lion* in 1928. This was recalled for the new *Lion* in 1961 and the College received the one formerly belonging to HMS *Queen Elizabeth*. It bears a London hallmark of 1801; the plate is engraved with Nelson's coat of arms, together with the Viscount's coronet awarded at the Battle of Copenhagen in April 1801.

Sports Trophy on Oak Base:
This trophy presented to the Wardroom Officers of HMS *Britannia* in 1888, consists of three figures depicting the sports of rugby, cricket and fencing surmounted by a naval crown held aloft by entwined dolphins.

1 The average length of appointment for a Naval Officer being two years probably accounts in part for the large number of silver items, as silver was a traditional gift to the Wardroom Mess.

Dormitory ventilation tower over A block.

Architect's original drawing of the headmaster's house, April 1905.

Tudor crown are finely carved in high relief on the surface of the oak lid. The interior of the casket, which contained the usual coins and records, was lined with royal blue velvet, and the whole was secured by a Chubb's patent lock actuated by a gold key of unusual design, introducing the acorn and oak leaves in reference to the 'wooden wall' from which the material was obtained. On the front of the casket was the following inscription:

> This casket, made from oak from HMS *Britannia*, was deposited in the foundation stone of the *Britannia* Royal Naval College by his Majesty King Edward VII, March 7, 1902.'

The descriptions of both caskets are very detailed and as such are likely to be accurate; *The Sphere* also carries a photograph of the wooden casket that matches its own description. It is therefore possible that there were two caskets interred at the ceremony, one from the Town of Dartmouth (the gilded and enamelled silver one) containing the loyal address, and the wooden one from the Navy containing the coins and papers. *The Sphere* carries an illustration with the Captain of *Britannia* handing coins and papers to the King, which would support this theory. The whole ceremony only lasted for one hour and fifteen minutes and the Royal Train departed for Plymouth at ten past four in the afternoon.

A Masterpiece of Edwardian Architecture

The College was initially designed by Aston Webb as a public school to replace the two hulks on the river. Public schools at the time reflected the architecture of the homes of the landed gentry, as the pupils, who were largely from the middle classes, aspired to be seen in a similar light (Wiener 1981 and Perkin 1990). The sons of the aristocracy almost invariably went to public schools, but the majority (and Dartmouth was no exception) were from middle class backgrounds (Kalton 1966). Dartmouth also conformed in its architecture, echoing the design of many English country houses at the time. The building's division into two wings either side of a central tower, its sweeping drives to the entrance and setting in open parkland all emulating the English country estate. The acquisition of the Raleigh estate also had its corollary in that many public schools sought to acquire surrounding lands from the gentry to protect their isolation. Indeed, Harrow School bought 220 acres for £90,000 in 1885 'to keep a distance from the rising tide of bricks and mortar'. This connection is also illustrated in the following passage from the Gieves 1935 booklet *How to become a Naval Officer, and Life at the Royal Naval College, Dartmouth*:

> 'As the officer goes from ship to ship and wardroom to wardroom he always feels at home; it is as if his quarters had been moved from another wing of the family mansion.'

Above: Crown and monogram surmount the hopper of a drainpipe. Such was Aston Webb's attention to architectural detail.

Right: Construction of D block, 1914-1917.

Below: Warship development carved in stone. These four prow models adorn the front of the building.

It is this visual analogy with aristocratic life that almost certainly determined the architect's thoughts when he designed his public school at Dartmouth. It reflected many of the great houses and public schools with the inclusion of a great hall, a central tower with dormitory and recreational wings either side. The proportions of the rooms and height of the ceilings were more than the average cadet would have been used to at home, the panelled and vaulted dining hall with its gallery was reminiscent of many Tudor or Elizabethan mansions. It is therefore not surprising that during his time as architect at Dartmouth, Aston Webb was also commissioned to design a war memorial for Harrow School (Colville 2003).

In spite of the above constraints and Aston Webb's reputation for being 'hopelessly eclectic' (Fellows 1995) the Royal Naval College is undeniably Edwardian in appearance. In his opening words Fellows (1995) describes 'the images of Edwardian architecture' as 'alluring: a lofty gable projecting high above the street, rising from a wall of warm red brick striped with creamy coloured stone; a richly craved frieze running below, a bay window framed in stone

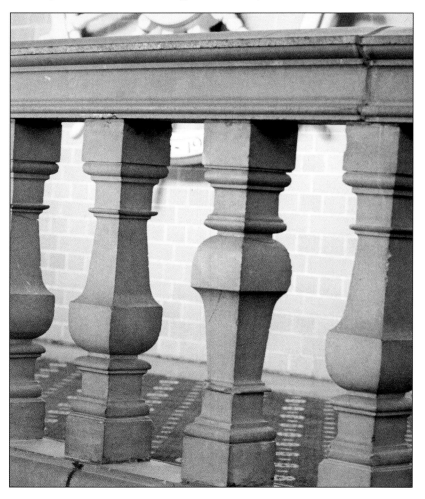

Architectural idiosyncrasy in the balustrades outside the Wardroom.

and set about with allegorical figures; over all a copper clad dome with lantern and gilded weather vane'. Except for the reference to rising above the street and the copper cladding of the dome, this description could very well refer to Dartmouth.

The site sits 180 feet above sea level and slopes steeply down to the River Dart, both to the south and to the east. Aston Webb accommodated the slope to the east by first choosing the site where the slope is less steep, and secondly by the use of stairs from the dining hall and the chapel. The main corridor is level, but at the eastern end there is a short flight of steps down to the level of the chapel and two short flights at the western end, leading up to the dining room. The slope to the south has resulted in the architect building the College as a series of terraces that are hardly obvious from the front elevation.

The parade ground, originally conceived as a sunken garden, is below the level of the thirty-foot wide main terrace. There are then steps into the main building, more steps to the main corridor, steps to the great hall and steps beyond to the buildings at the rear of the great hall, the entire building being a series of levels rising to the north. The College was originally designed to accommodate 260 cadets with dormitories and recreation rooms in the two wings (now known as A & B blocks) and classrooms off the great hall (now known as the quarterdeck). However, after the announcement of Lord Selborne's scheme there were to be 390 cadets in six terms of sixty-five each. The College was therefore inadequate for the intended numbers, a situation that has plagued Dartmouth ever since the College was built. To accommodate this increased number, an extra accommodation block was added at the time of building at right angles to the chapel (now known as C block), with its own sanitary annexe. The sick quarters were opened in 1902, a sign that the health of the cadets was still of great concern to the Admiralty. These quarters consisted of sixty-four beds, forty for infectious and twenty-four for non-infectious cases, these were in three isolated two-storey wings. In addition there are nurses quarters at one end and a day-room and administrative block at the other. The block also boasts operating rooms and a dispensary, in addition to a large house for the doctor[5]. Since the 1960s the old doctor's house has been the residence of the Commander of the College.

The fresh water supply for the College was originally taken from a spring at Sandquay and pumped to a reservoir situated one hundred feet above the College; this fed a large cistern in the clock tower, which fed the entire College. The salt water supply for the swimming pool was pumped from the river and this also fed the plunge baths and the hydrants. The heating for the College was from a boiler and engine house at Sandquay, and this reached the College via a service duct, which in recent years has been the roost of

5 The first patient in the new hospital was Cadet C W Graham, who broke his leg in the first game of the 1902-3 season, 'quite a proper and appropriate baptism' the *Britannia Magazine* reported. Fatalities were not uncommon and on 11th June 1904 Cadet Boycott died at the hospital.

The Commodore's house.

and transported to the College site via a narrow gauge rope hauled tramway. A small quarry was opened at Sandquay that was used to supply local stone for the boundary walling. Some sand for building purposes was removed from a small beach near Stoke Gabriel, a few miles up river.

The interior of the chapel combines Bath Stone with the red bricks that dominate the exterior. The high vaulted ceiling above the chancel show this feature to good effect, while the roof of the main aisle has a wooden beamed roof with delicately carved cherubs on the main bosses of the beam work. Originally the chapel was illuminated by electroliers similar to those in the main dining room (Senior Gunroom), but with cherubs as the main theme. It is traditional for the chapels of public schools and colleges to have the seating running longitudinally, facing each other, but here Aston Webb broke with tradition and somewhat controversially for the time, placed the seating across the main body of the chapel, as would be found in a traditional church.

The chapel displays a wide variety of decorative marble work, this was entrusted to the local company of H. T. Jenkins and Son, of Torquay. This reflected Aston Webb's desire to use local materials whenever possible. To help with the marble work, four stonemasons were brought over from Italy, all of whom settled in Dartmouth, their descendants living locally today. Their work was not only confined to the College, several shop doorways in Dartmouth still show evidence of their skills.

The twelve-foot high marble panelling in the chancel is Italian in origin and has been cut and opened out to give a very striking pattern, the colouring subtly changing to become lighter nearer to the altar, signifying the transition 'from darkness into light'. In between these panels are columns of local Devonian limestone from Jenkins' Kingsley quarry and in the panel at the top are decorations of a green marble, which is possibly from Connemara in western Ireland. The chancel floor is laid with a dark veined variety of marble and white Cararra marble from Italy, while the

The College nearing completion, with the headmaster's house still only partially built. The inclined ropeway and temporary jetty, used during construction, are clearly visible (Dartmouth Museum).

side ambones are of beautiful deep red Victoria marble from Cork. The steps to the chancel, the altar rail step, and the plinths to both the ambones and the altar are all of locally quarried dark Devonian limestone (known as Ashburton marble and from Jenkins' quarries) close examination will reveal fossil corals within.

The above is a description of the College as it opened in 1905, with the Master's Hostel and the swimming pool opening the following year. However, as in the past fluctuations in the student population, due to changes in entry regulations and the demands of the fleet for new officers, was soon to apply pressure on the available accommodation. It was therefore only two years before the first substantial extension was opened in 1907. This has always been known as E Block, and has for more than forty years contained the Chapel of the Church of Scotland and Free Churches. (The Chapel celebrated its 40th anniversary in 2003). The rest of the Block now houses the computer training rooms.

Further Expansion of the College

The first major extension was the addition of what is now known as D Block, which was completed in 1917. In the years after the College was opened there was an increasing requirement for more naval officers. This demand was to be met in part by the introduction of the 'Special Entry' for boys who had previously completed an education at public school. Nevertheless, the total expected entry to the Naval College of 110 per term was almost

double that of 1905, which clearly required additional accommodation. The result was an entirely new block, to be constructed to the north of the original main buildings, and to house an extra dining room (now called the Junior Gunroom), three large gunrooms for recreational purposes and more dormitory space, in addition to more studies (classrooms) and a Common Room for the Masters. Aston Webb's practice in London was awarded the contract, although it has been suggested by Davies and Grove (1980) that he no longer controlled the work there at that time. It is also a popular myth that upon seeing the completed extension and the scar on the skyline view of the original College, that he washed his hands of Dartmouth and was never to return. There is however no evidence at all to support this view, and it is believed by some students of architecture to be pure speculation. Aston Webb was sixty-five years of age when these works were started in the summer of 1914 and he may have not have been as involved as he was in the original building. However, it was only three years earlier that he was responsible designing and overseeing the building of Admiralty Arch in London. How much the architect was involved in the design of D Block we shall probably never know, but when viewed from the south it does bear more than a passing resemblance to the façade of Buckingham Palace, a project which was his entirely. The arrangement of terraced and mezzanine floors in the original building is continued through into D Block, at least in keeping with Aston Webb's original theme. The construction is of red brick and Portland stone, just as in the original College, but it is of

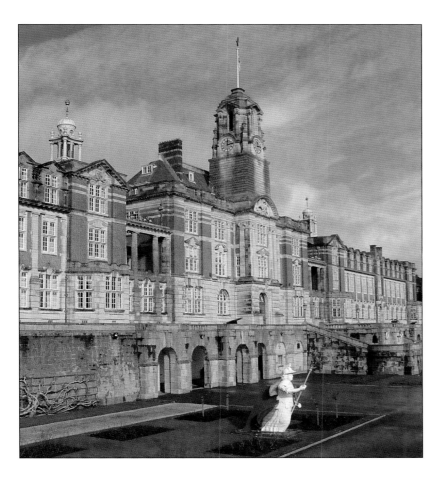

The College as it approaches its centenary.

a much more utilitarian design, probably reflecting its wartime period of building. There are few Portland stone courses to relieve the vast area of brick, and the front elevation is flat, in contrast to that of the original College, which is relieved with projecting gables and bays. It has a flat roof unlike the original 1905 building with its lofty slate clad, hipped and gabled roofs. The new block does have an imposing entrance with a Portland stone gable, above it at roof height, is an elaborately carved royal coat of arms[7]. Nevertheless, while the lower floors do possess elaborate large windows with gracefully curved upper portions and ornate brickwork, mirroring that at the rear of the main building which this block faces, the two upper floors are flat and without relief. Unfortunately it is only the two upper floors that are visible from a distance, as the original building hides the more elaborate lower floors. The upper floors were completed towards the end of the first world war, and wartime shortages of both materials and labour may be the reason why the upper two floors are much more austere than the lower floors.

Although the lower floors do bear all the hallmarks of Aston Webb design it is likely that he did not design the upper two floors. New studies were completed in May 1917 that also joined the new block to the existing building, which itself was opened in September of that year.

Aston Webb's magnificent College suffered bomb damage in 1942[8], but only makeshift repairs could be carried out because of wartime shortages of labour and materials. Repairs were started after the war and were completed in time for the return of the cadets to the College in September 1946. Also in that year, the foundations were laid for a new building to accommodate areas for the teaching of the new additions to the curriculum, music and art. This brick building of utilitarian design is rectangular, and flat-roofed, but functional, reflecting the modern outlook of the time. Fortunately it is hidden behind D Block, and so does not detract from the fine proportions of the original 1905 building, nor indeed the 1917 D Block. Its large open rooms, originally intended for music and art are now used for classes in navigation, it also houses the College's modern 'Bridge Trainer' *Daring*. The building, now referred to as F Block, is the Navigation Department Block.

The major changes in training as a result of the COST Committee report[9], saw the College cease to be a naval public school and become a naval training college for naval officers. This had major implications for the building. A sub-committee was set up in June 1954 to examine the necessary works and buildings that would be required. It was decided at an early stage that COST's solution of providing extra instructional and living accommodation by putting up standard Ministry of Supply buildings was out of the question. As far as the Navy was concerned, Dartmouth was an ancient monument and so must not be spoilt. Throughout the discussions and subsequent planning, thought was given to keeping the buildings viewed from the south, the main aspect of the building, 'architecturally in accord with the existing buildings'. Fortunately the need for this was also recognised by the Treasury.

The first major change was to be in sleeping accommodation, where the existing dormitories on the first and second floors were to be altered into single cabin accommodation for the midshipmen and four berth cabins for cadets. It was felt that the cadets would more easily be acclimatised to communal life in non-single cabins, a belief that remains the case today. The house or divisional system was to continue and therefore the gunrooms only changed in how they were used. They became purely recreational spaces instead of working/recreational spaces, and hence only the furnishings were altered. The report recommended that midshipmen should enjoy a higher 'standard of elegance' in their messing, so it became necessary for the midshipmen and cadets to mess separately, leading

---

7 This carving was originally on the exterior of the northern gable of the great hall (quarterdeck), it being removed to this position when D Block was built.

8 See Chapter 5 The College at War.

9 See Chapter 6 Education, 1945-2005.

to the reactivation of the D Block mess and galley. This necessitated a great deal of work in both messes (dining halls) and galleys. These two messes became the Junior Gunroom for the cadets (juniors) and the Senior Gunroom for the seniors, these arrangements continue to this day. A separate bar and billiard room was set up in the gunroom nearest to the seniors dining hall (Senior Gunroom), and it remains to this day as a television room.

The Wardroom, which was originally built to house about twenty-five officers, became quite inadequate for the new role, as officer numbers were expected to rise to fifty or more. As an extension was necessary, it was decided to make possible the provision of a combined mess of which officers and lecturers could be full members. As stated in the Captain's report of the time 'cohesion between the Service and Civilian staff has always been desirable but under the new scheme it is even more essential and this seemed a good way of helping it on'. (Captain's Report of the COST Scheme Recommendations. – College Archive). The Wardroom extension that followed displaced a number of storerooms; hence a new victualling block was built, incorporating some victualling offices and a Catering Officers Flat (this is now known as the Wardroom Flat). The extension to the Wardroom and the alterations to the Senior Gunroom resulted in a major refurbishment of the attached galleys. This resulted in a movement of one of the large doors from the Senior Gunroom to the galley. The work was skilfully executed and the original wooden panelling was taken out and replaced with great care. The only evidence of the move is that the carved names of the battles and admirals at the top of the panelling are now out of date sequence in two of the panels.

Other building work involved the building of a new annexe to D Block, containing additional cabins, to accommodate the increased numbers with the COST scheme. The firm of Stanbury of Plymouth was to be the main contractor for all the new works. A new lecture hall was included in the original plan, but the Treasury did not sanction its building at this stage. Other moves involved the clothing store moving from D Block to C wing of the old hospital, recently vacated by the Admiralty Interview Board.

The College would have to wait almost ten years to get the new lecture hall originally suggested in the COST scheme, and this was to be the last major new building to date. The impetus for the commencement of building of the new hall was the 'Unison 63' conference to be held at Dartmouth in September 1963. This was a gathering of Commonwealth armed forces and was planned by Lord Mountbatten as Chief of Defence Staff. It was to be a multi-purpose building seating 485, intended for lectures, discussions, cinema and theatrical shows, musical recitals (previously held in the chapel or gymnasium) and examinations. It was for the latter that the removable tip-up seating was installed. It is used for a wide variety of purposes but not examinations, latterly the gymnasium was used, but now with small groups sitting classrooms are used. The sloping site suited the building well, as the architects could make use of the slope for the raked seating. The architects Messrs Playne, Lacy and Partners of Westminster, were appointed; they now incorporated the practice of Sir Aston Webb and Son, the original architect for the College, producing an unbroken line from 1905 to 1963. The building is in red brick with a broad Portland stone band at the top, so as to harmonise with the other College buildings. The building has a cinema projection room over a generously proportioned entrance foyer, with cloakrooms. It is apparent that when built it was for a predominantly all male college population, as the ladies' facilities are totally inadequate – ask any lady who has ever needed to make use of them. The hall has a generous stage made of maple some twenty feet in depth, with changing rooms beneath. The main auditorium has a suspended ceiling and its back wall is treated acoustically; the plain plaster walls have a beech veneer dado and the entrance foyer an attractive terrazzo floor. The hall was first used by Admiral of the Fleet Sir Casper John[10] to address the young officers' passing out in the summer of 1963. The hall was named *Casper John Hall* in his honour, an act that may have been thought insensitive as it was Lord Mountbatten who provided initial impetus to its building. 'Unison 63' took place in the September of that year, when there were 220 representatives from twelve nations.

It is perhaps therefore fitting that the last major building at Dartmouth should be designed by Messrs Playne and Lacy and Partners, the company that incorporated the practice of the original architect of the college, Sir Aston Webb. One hundred years since the doors on Aston Webb's masterpiece opened to its first term of cadets, it continues to symbolise the pride and traditions of the Royal Navy.

10 Casper John was christened in the College chapel in March 1918. His father was the artist Augustus John, who had no obvious naval connections, and why the ceremony took place at Dartmouth remains a mystery.

The College Library

*T*he College Library can trace its origins to the shelves of leather spined books lining the deckheads of the hulks moored in the Dart. Indeed many of those books still line the shelves of the present library, providing a tangible link with the past.

Upon opening, the College did not have a central library, one having not been called for during design. Instead, there were scattered collections, such as the Common Room reference library, the cadets' reference library and the cadets' lending library, together with others, reflecting specific interests, such as those for the Field, Art and Music Clubs. These were finally consolidated into one location in 1933, when accommodation was made available in what is now the Lower Library, toward the rear of O Block. This was enlarged to encompass three former classrooms on the Upper level upon the College's return to Dartmouth in 1946.

Prior to 1955, the library was in essence a school library, designed to meet the needs of a public school, albeit with a slightly unusual curriculum. During this period, the task of Librarian was performed part-time by a member of the History and English Department, most notable of which in the post war period being Cyril Barnes-Lawrence, who held the post from 1928 to 1958. He was followed by Captain Pack, author of the former standard College history, Britannia at Dartmouth. However, as the College continued its transformation into a tertiary educational training establishment, demand

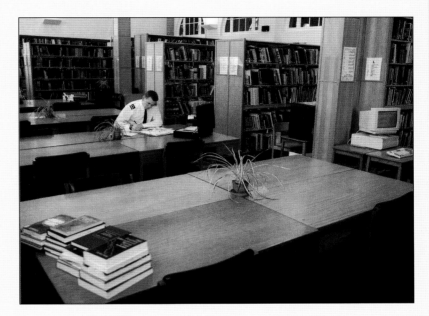

A student at work in the lower library.

grew for the post to be upgraded to full time. The first professional librarian was Graham White, appointed in 1964. He was followed in 1974 by Michael Chapman and in 1977 by the present incumbent, Richard Kennell. Staffing now consists of a Librarian, a Deputy and an Assistant.

Today, the library fulfills several functions, whilst providing a quiet study space amidst the bustle of college life. It boasts a substantial book-stock of some 61,000 volumes, subscriptions to almost 200 journals, around 1,500 videos and DVDs as well as CD ROMs. Access to the Internet is also provided. Primarily, the library exists to support the core educational and training function. However, its breadth of coverage also supports many recreational and historical pursuits, including research by students from local universities, authors and historians, who utilise the particular blend of historical resources, built up over the years. These have been augmented by material gleaned from many closed establishments, beginning with RNC Osborne and most recently RNC Greenwich.

As the College Library enters the twenty-first century, its primary role in support of student learning and development is being challenged by changes in the syllabus and the availability of electronic sources. However, it would be difficult to completely replace the vast collection of knowledge contained on the shelves. Similarly, it would be hard to replace the sense of shared history experienced when consulting a book which may have been thumbed by George VI, Mountbatten, Leach or Lewin and what is more, within the environment in which they did it.

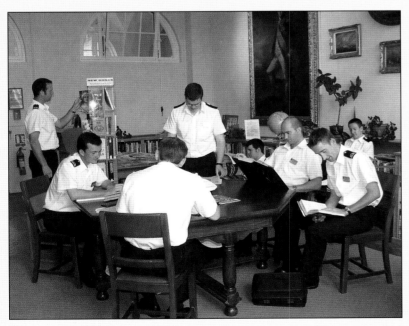

A group of students enjoying the resources of the upper library.

up to the age of thirteen.' (Ibid. p.468) The interview board, consisting of naval officers, including a captain, and a headmaster, was designed to assess the general suitability of the boy, aided by a report from the boy's headmaster. The examination which followed the approval of the First Sea Lord as to the boy's suitability, aimed to ensure a level of academic ability. The exam, which 'seems to have been of an enlightened nature for those days.' (Pack 1966, p.148) was divided into two parts. The first consisted of tests in English, history, geography, French or German, arithmetic, algebra, and geometry; in the second part there was a choice between Latin, another modern language, or an essay question in science. The objective was to allow open competition, enabling the best possible candidates to come forward. The reality was, however, that most boys 'were simply not able to take advantage of the new system. Their parents lacked the financial resources to put them through the private education system.' (Davies 2003, p.25) For Dartmouth was a public school, run by the Navy; its pupils were not yet in the Navy, but the sole purpose of the school was to provide the Navy with specially educated boys who would become the officers of the future. Fisher himself had reservations about charging fees for a naval education (a sum of £75 per annum plus cost of uniform and other kit and equipment), restricting the pool of 'future Nelsons,' but the system was in fact designed to catch a particular type of boy from a particular middle to upper class background. The aim to abolish the class distinction between the executive and engineering branches, as claimed by an Admiralty memorandum from 1905 (Kemp 1964, p.159) should be more accurately interpreted as attempting to draw both from the same class, rather than extending entry to the lower classes.

Having successfully passed the selection procedure cadets would spend four years at the Royal Naval College. During this time, as Professor Ewing explained in 1906, they would 'receive a general education on modern lines which should include an exceptionally large element of practical science and engineering.' (Kemp 1964, p.174) The curriculum which, according to Ewing, would resemble that of 'a good public school,' covered instruction in 'mathematics, heat, electricity; in the science and practice of engineering; in French [plus German for the more able], English composition and literature; in history, both general and naval; in geography, navigation and the elements of seamanship; and in religious knowledge.' A good deal of time would also be spent in workshops, including instruction in 'carpentering and pattern making, in turning, moulding and casting, in blacksmithing and coppersmithing, and in mechanical drawing.' (Ibid. p.179) The result was to provide 'an education for the boy who is to become a man of action, not a philosopher.' (Ibid. p.180)

Inevitably, given the extent of the reforms being proposed, Fisher and Selborne were met with criticism and opposition for their scheme. As Fisher wrote in 1904, 'in our recent naval revolution in regard to entry and education of officers, all the senior officers of the Navy were against it to a man! *Never were such bitter things said!*' (Marder 1953, p.301) Selborne too admitted to 'some bad "quarters of an hour" in reconciling conflicting views and interests…' at the Admiralty (Boyce 1990, p.152). Fisher was driven to exclaim, 'I am not sure the "training of our Admirals" is not equally pressing with the 'training of our Midshipmen'!'. (Marder 1953, p.255) Objections centred round the common training of executive and engineer officers. Much of

Hobbies: model aircraft club.

Attentive cadets at study in a classroom in the 1920s.

POWER HOUSE

R.N. COLLEGE. DARTMOUTH.

Engineering instruction in the powerhouse at Sandquay.

the detractor's opposition seems to have been based on sheer snobbery, not wishing to 'taint the glory of the executive officer with the oil, grime, and heat of the engine-room.' (Mackay 1973, p.277)[3] Indeed *The Times* journalist James Thursfield[4], wrote to Fisher telling him of a conversation with Lord Spencer who had been approached by 'a distinguished person' to lead an attack on the scheme. When Lord Spencer refused to do so, the anonymous 'great man' replied; *'Are you prepared to defend our officers going down in the coal hole?'* (Marder 1953, p.268) But underlying this there was a genuine concern about 'interchangeablity' between the branches reducing the degree of specialist knowledge on board ship. The intention, however, was merely to give deck officers sufficient engineering and scientific knowledge to understand the workings of their ships and weapons systems, while providing engineers (and Marines) with an appreciation of the art of seamanship, thus creating the 'lifelong community of sentiment' Fisher wished to establish. (Penn 2000, p.88) In so doing, however, there was the danger that the specialist engineer would

lack the technical knowledge of his predecessors. For Fisher, though, this was to miss the point as 'all are going to be educated as Engineer Officers from their first entry...we only want a Faraday and a George Stephenson about every two or three years.' (Marder 1953, p.269)

Not all contemporary opinion was against the Fisher-Selborne scheme. The Prince of Wales, a former *Britannia* cadet, wrote to Fisher:

'I call it a grand scheme and wish it every success. No doubt it will be severely criticised by the old ones, who are too conservative for our modern days ... I am certain the Navy will greatly benefit by having your Engineer and Marine officers drawn from the same class as your Executive officers ...' (Ibid. p.266-7)

3 It was often said of engineers that it had taken an act of Parliament to make them officers, but it would take an act of God to make them gentlemen.

4 Fisher was adept at using the media to promote his ideas and rewarded those who supported him with privileged information. *The Times* journalist James Thursfield was the most privileged amongst this group.

Still Life.

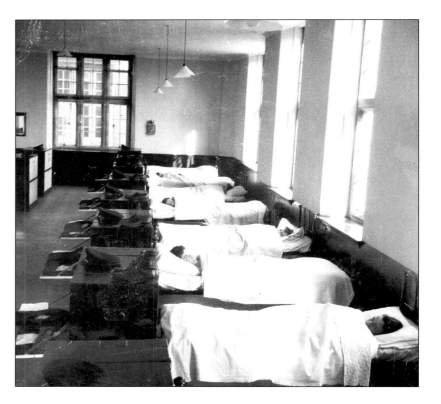

And so to bed.

Even Admiral Lord Charles Beresford, with whom Fisher was later to fall out over his war plans, described the scheme as 'a brilliant and statesmanlike effort to grapple with *a problem upon the sound settlement of which depends the future efficiency of the British Navy.'* (Fisher 1919, p.167) Indeed by the time the scheme was published, Fisher was to claim that it had been *'the unanimous decision of the whole Board of the Admiralty ...'* (Ibid. p.267) He went on in 1904 to write:

'Now they all see an immense success looming in the distance, magnifying the efficiency of the Navy beyond any present conception, and all hands are beginning to "Hosanna," when a year ago they wanted to "crucify"!' (Ibid. p.302)

The real proof, of course, would come when the first naval cadets entered under the new system.

Two New Naval Colleges

The reduction in the age of entry and subsequent lengthening of the course meant that it would take longer for a new cadet to be added to the active list than under the old *Britannia* system. The new College being built at Dartmouth had been designed for the existing, shorter (two year rather than four year) course and was therefore of insufficient size to take all new scheme cadets. Moreover, the building was not going to be ready for completion until 1905. It was therefore decided to look for an additional college, which

could be made ready to receive its first cadets by September 1903. The solution was found through the bequest from King Edward VII of his parents' home on the Isle of White, Osborne House. The main house was to be used as a convalescence home for service men but the stable block was converted to provide gunrooms and classrooms for a new naval college. The stables, together with a number of additional huts, were therefore hurriedly constructed within seven months to become the Royal Naval College, Osborne. Cadets would subsequently spend two years at Osborne, before progressing to the extended senior college at Dartmouth[5]. The first cadets to make the transition arrived at Britannia Royal Naval College on September 14th 1905. Meanwhile, the old *Britannia* system, with the older entry was to run concurrently with the new system for two and a half years, in order to maintain the flow of officers into the service. The architects of the new scheme were determined to ensure that there would be as little influence as possible from the old scheme. Captain Cross, the last Captain of *Britannia*, was thus most disappointed to be denied command of what he had originally regarded as his College. When both groups of cadets entered the new College in September 1905, it was ensured that the new schemers would outnumber the old, an additional two of the *Britannia* terms having been sent off to complete their training at sea.

5 See Chapter 2 Architecture.

Initial impressions of the new scheme from those involved were positive. Captain Rosslyn Wemyss, the first captain of Osborne felt sure that '… these young gentlemen will turn out more capable all-round officers than the present generation of young officers at sea.' (Kemp 1964, p.165) While Captain Goodenough, the first captain of Dartmouth was satisfied that instruction in engineering and science at an early age had '… in no way taken from the cadets their independence of character or boyish enthusiasm. It has in reality much increased those qualities and the somewhat more strenuous life they lead in comparison with other schools has in every way brought out the best points of the boys character.' (Ibid. p.167) The only serious reservation held by both was that boys were being discouraged from opting to take engineering as their specialisation.

One of the initial problems encountered at the new naval colleges was to combine naval and academic organisation with a captain and a headmaster. However, as Ewing observed; 'thanks to the good sense and good feeling of the persons concerned and to the constant desire, which all share, to make the College effective for their purpose, these difficulties are surmountable.' (Kemp 1964, p.180) Indeed, such was to remain the case, save but a few exceptions, until the academic community at Dartmouth was integrated with the naval staff, under a Commander Naval Education and Training, in 2004.

In another of his perceptive appointments, Fisher had bestowed the position of Headmaster of Osborne to Cyril Ashford, senior science master at Harrow School. On the completion by the first new scheme entry of their two years at Osborne, Ashford was to join them as Headmaster of Dartmouth. His comments were once again essentially positive, dismissing a number of the concerns previously raised, and emphasising the public school mould in which Osborne and Dartmouth were formed:

'I have no hesitation in saying that the broader education now given will immensely increase the officer's control over his men and his power of getting the best work out of the subordinate engine-room artificers.

'… the fact that the future engineer officer will have studied the subjects considered the province of the executive officer who specialises in torpedo work, will set him on a plane above his men; it is proverbial in civil life that a public schoolboy, although in most cases grossly ignorant of all scientific matters, makes a better works-manager than the more highly trained product of the technical schools, if the education and social environment of the latter man has been bounded by that limited horizon. I believe I am right in saying that the personal qualities which are developed by a non-specialised education in an atmosphere such as that of Osborne or the more strenuous of the old public schools, are more valuable in claiming respect in the engine-room of a battleship than in a factory. The well-educated English boy of the upper classes possesses sanctions of conduct that lie outside the mental equipment of a man who has devoted his time to the perfection of his manual, or even his exclusively scientific powers … In part, no doubt, these qualities which shine out in emergencies are the results of

Pen and ink sketch by Frank Wood of the Officers' quarters and mast at the RNC Osborne, 1908.

heredity and home influence … but the public school system of England is sadly at fault if they are not in part due to education in the humanities and to the companionship, during the formative years of youth, of other boys who are being trained to command their fellow men by all agencies, even games, that have been found effective. This education and these agencies are an integral factor of the new scheme, and I venture to assure that in these respects Osborne is inferior to no public school both in the appreciation of their importance which is possessed by those in control, and in the enthusiasm with which the cadets take advantage of the opportunities.' (Ibid. p.173)

It is apparent from Ashford's comments that he regarded a good general education along the lines of the best public schools as more than adequate compensation for greater scientific or technical instruction. This was not necessarily the case in Fisher's mind, having originally intended for half rather than a third of cadets' time to have been spent on engineering. As he wrote in his memoirs in 1919;

'… we wanted "Machinery Education," both with officers and men; and also that education should be the education of common sense. My full idea of Osborne was alas! emasculated by the schoolmasters of the nation.' (Fisher 1919, p.123)

Again the suggestion is that the equality aimed at was to take all officers from the same class thus ending class distinction between branches, rather than opening up opportunities for boys of all classes to become naval officers.

The aim to provide more officers for the service, however, remained only partially fulfilled. Consequently in 1913 First Lord of the Admiralty Winston Churchill introduced the Special Entry scheme. Under this system boys aged between seventeen and a half and eighteen and a half that had completed their education at a public school, could join the Navy as cadets for a six-month course on board a training ship, initially HMS *Highflyer*. By admitting more mature boys who had received a non-naval based general education the Special Entry scheme ran counter to some of the core principles

Meal time in the Senior Gun Room.

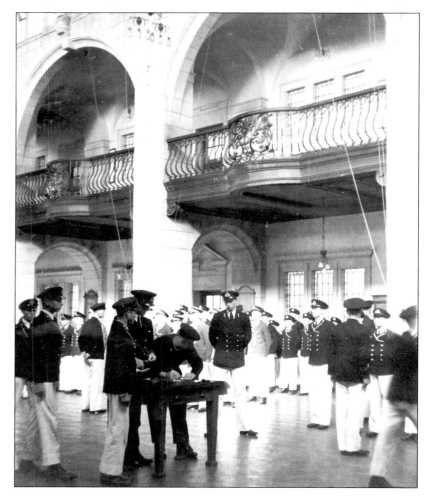

Receiving pocket money on the Quarterdeck.

Seamanship instruction in rope work. This room is currently the E-learning centre.

of the Selborne Scheme. Nevertheless, the two systems were to run concurrently until the thirteen-year-old entry was abolished after the Second World War. During that time both systems were to produce their share of competent officers, with Special Entry at times providing more officers than Dartmouth.[6]

From War to Peace to War Again

Nine years after the first cadets arrived at Dartmouth from Osborne the long anticipated conflict with Germany finally broke out. The response at Dartmouth was swift and decisive. The entire College was mobilized for war on August 1st 1914, sending cadets, most of whom had yet to complete their training, into the

fleet. Although students did arrive from Osborne in September 1914 numbers at the College were to fluctuate throughout the war, depending on the need for officers at sea.[7]

The end of the war was to be the cause of even greater disruption. By 1920 the combination of peace and economic stringency had led to the 'Geddes axe', cutting throughout the Navy. In addition to reducing the entry into the Naval Colleges there was also to be a forty per cent reduction among the existing terms at Osborne and Dartmouth. On the whole these reductions seem to have been voluntary and less drastic than originally feared (Davis & Grove 1980, p. 15). However, with the reduction in the number of cadets there was now enough room to accommodate them in one rather than two colleges. With its still largely temporary buildings and poor health record, Osborne was the natural casualty. In May 1920 two terms from Osborne started to move to Dartmouth. One year later the remaining

6 According to John Beattie, in the period 1913-55 about half the officers in the Royal Navy (including Paymasters, Mates and Upper Yardmen) were not entered to the College as 13 and 16 year old entries. Of the Flag Officers in the 1970s 50% were Special Entries, 25% Darts, 25% from other routes.

7 For a full account of the impact of both World Wars on BRNC see Chapter 5, The College at War.

College Sport

'*With the re-opening of the College on September 11th all our thoughts were at once concentrated — on the River in preparation for the coming Regatta.*' This quotation from the Britannia Magazine of Christmas 1915 underlines how highly sport at BRNC was regarded, one might have thought that 'our thoughts' should have been with those former cadets who were on active service, but alas no, sport was uppermost in the editor's thoughts. After all the College was a public school and sport has always been a major part of public school life. In previous histories of HMS Britannia and the College such as Statham (1904), Hughes (1950) and Pack (1966) the progress of the cricket and rugby football teams have featured, given almost as high a priority as the major historical events chronicled by the authors. One of the criteria in choosing a location for the old Britannia was the availability of level land for use as playing fields in the locality. The College has always offered a wide range of sporting activities as the sports trophy cabinet can testify, the sports of sailing and rowing remaining as popular today as they were in the days of the old Britannia.

Cricket has always been one of the main sports enjoyed at the College, and the importance attached

Swimming regatta.

The *Britannia* team that played against W. G. Grace and the MCC in 1889.

to it is shown by the fact that in the days of the old Britannia two cricket professionals were employed. One was a professional groundsman to look after the 'square' on the playing fields, but the other was the professional coach; in 1889 this was a Mr Underwood, who coached the boys until the summer of 1893. In July 1889 a two-day match was organized between HMS Britannia and the MCC. W. G. Grace[1] captained the MCC team and Lt Abdy of HMS Britannia, who had played with W. G. at Lord's, arranged the match. W. G. only played for the second day as he had agreed to play at Bristol for Gloucestershire against the Gentlemen of Philadelphia. On the first day Britannia had to follow on, scoring only sixty-one against the MCC's 156 and they won by seven wickets. W. G. did not arrive until the evening of the first day so another game was played on the second day. In the second match the MCC went in first and declared at 118 for two wickets. W. G. made forty-eight before being bowled out. In reply Britannia's boys made eighty-two for nine wickets, W G taking seven of them. The local paper reported that the 'cadets fielded very well', when in fact they had a very good match indeed against one of England's top sides, used to making high scores and taking their fair share of wickets in

'Assault at Arms' summer of 1906.

top class cricket. By 1902 the cadets had a cricket professional again, by the name of Lord, and the playing fields were maintained to a very high standard. It was Wellington who said that 'the Battle of Waterloo was won on the playing fields of Eton'. The Admiralty funded the upkeep of the playing fields so that the Navy had no excuse for not winning their victories on the cricket fields of Dartmouth.

Rugby football was the main winter sport and matches were reported with the same enthusiasm as was shown for cricket matches, especially in the Britannia Magazine. One former cadet who joined HMS Britannia in 1902 is immortalized at the home of English Rugby at Twickenham where his name is proudly displayed on the honours board. That was Arthur Leyland Harrison who gained two international caps while playing for the United Services team against Ireland and France in the 1913-14 season. He is better known at Dartmouth as the recipient of the Victoria Cross that is on display in the College.[2]

In 1897 the sport of hockey was introduced and matches of Cadet Captains v Ship; Officers v Ship and Britannia v Hindostan, were to become features of the sporting field. Beagling was introduced in the winter of 1878/9, as reported elsewhere in

Tug of war at New Entry sports on the Parade Ground.

this book, as a sport for those cadets who were less competitive in the more traditional sports. Indeed, the sporting programme remained varied. Clay pigeon shooting was introduced by Captain Cross, the last Captain of the Britannia *and remains a popular sport today. Another sporting tradition at Dartmouth is the cross-country race, this is a regular event in*

which all cadets take part; the pain of running up 'Britannia Steps' still etched on many a former cadet or young officer's mind. This event dates back to the days of the old Britannia *and was run across the surrounding farmland, but today it merely takes in a circuit of the College grounds.*

The river has always played a major part in the activities at Dartmouth and sailing and rowing have always been popular pastimes, for both recreational and sporting pursuits. The College maintains a large quantity of craft, which includes boats for practical seamanship instruction and as well for pleasure and sport. Many former members of the College will remember 'away all boats', when all the College would walk down to Sandquay and take part in a scratch race, that in effect was an exercise in seamanship against the clock. The College has also had a close association with the Port of Dartmouth and always taken part in the annual Port of Dartmouth Royal Regatta.

The College also boasts a nine-hole golf course for the use of the young officers and staff. The College grounds occupy approximately 117 acres of which about thirty eight can be regarded as parkland.[3] This parkland was at one time leased to a local farmer as grazing. This provided a pleasant pastoral scene but did necessitate the use of an ugly wire fence around the establishment. In 1965 it was decided to turn this parkland into a golf course. The work was started at the beginning of the summer term, with cadets providing the labour, the youngest of whom, P. St. A. Sweet was given the privilege of cutting the first sod. A start was made on the third green as this was considered to be one of the two most difficult, and the insistence of the farmer that machinery must not be taken over his precious pasture, made it particularly hard work. It soon became apparent that the voluntary system of labour would not be sufficient for the task in hand, so each division was given a green and asked to finish it by

the end of term, so that the greens could be sown in the autumn. The value of golf as an officer's sport was recognized prior to the Second World War when a golf professional used to attend once a week and give tuition on Norton Fields. In 1965 the College paid for a block subscription to Thurlestone Golf Club, but as first year cadets were not allowed cars at the College the sport of golf was denied to them. As the ground available for the course was limited, future players ought to be masters of the 'short game,' however it was possible to include two long holes. Initially the greens had to be fenced, because of the farmer and his grazing, but today one can enjoy a round without the obstacle of the fences and appreciate the magnificent views of Dartmouth.

Sport at Dartmouth remains very much a part of College life and Wednesday and Saturday afternoons are traditionally set aside for the young officers to participate in their chosen sporting activity. The College also has strong sporting links with both the Army and Royal Air Force initial training establishments and games weekends against both the Royal Military Academy Sandhurst and RAF Cranwell are still regular features of the College sporting calendar.

For the high jump!

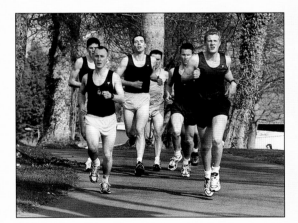

Running the cross-country.

1. W. G. Grace had family connections in South Devon and in January 1890, his son H. E. Grace joined HMS *Britannia*, as a cadet.

2. Arthur Leyland Harrison was born in Torquay and was awarded the VC for his part in commanding the Naval storming parties at Zeebrugge on 22nd-23rd April 1918, losing his life in that action. His brother Percy Harrison was a master at the Royal Naval College Osborne, but he came out of retirement to teach at Dartmouth during the Second World War as there was a shortage of teaching staff, many being on active service.

3 The College for many years kept a horse named Daisy whose primary task was to keep the parkland mown. She was a feature of the College for many years and in the winter, when she would otherwise be under-utilized she was loaned to a local farmer.

four terms moved to Dartmouth, along with the first new entries to join Dartmouth directly since the end of the old *Britannia* system. Captain Marten had been appointed captain of Osborne during the College's last term and transferred to Dartmouth with the last of the Osborne cadets to become Captain of Dartmouth.

The 1920s at Dartmouth have been described by Davies and Grove as a 'Golden Age', by Pack as 'Halcyon Days', while Hughes remembered the period between the wars as 'in many ways the happiest.' (1950, p.89) Indeed, having successfully integrated the junior and senior colleges into eleven Dartmouth terms, staff and students settled into a regular and comfortable regime. The curriculum had already changed in 1921 when the amount of engineering instruction was cut by two-thirds, 'to be treated less from the vocational and more from the educational standpoint.' (Ibid. p.96) Henceforth, sufficient engineer officers could be obtained voluntarily from the Special Entry, enabling all Dartmouth cadets to become executive officers, unless they chose otherwise.

With the arrival of the Osborne cadets Ashford introduced a number of special courses to broaden cadets' interest. For one period a week they could follow courses covering a variety of subjects from astronomy and Greek art to archaeology and architecture. Cadets at Dartmouth had always been encouraged to develop hobbies and pastimes to occupy their leisure time. Numerous clubs and societies existed as a browse though the *Britannia Magazine* from the early part of the twentieth century shows, with reports of the clubs' activities often appearing with both photographic and artistic contributions submitted by the cadets.

Music often played a large part in the life of the boys with both a band and choir performing regularly. The band in summer term of 1917 had fifty-five members, of whom forty-two were cadets, the rest being from the college staff (masters and naval officers and one Chief Petty Officer). The instruments played were varied in both number and variety, for example eighteen banjo players, five clarinets, six mandolins, six violins and a variety of other instruments including bassoon, trombone, timpani, euphonium and glockenspiel, under the supervision of the conductors Mr Piggot[8] and Mr Ovenden. The band would perform concerts for the cadets and play for the regular Saturday evening dances. There was also an active choir with thirty cadets regularly attending choir practice in the summer of 1917, all again under the direction of Mr Piggott, with Mr Ovenden playing the organ. The cadets made up the trebles and alto sections with the staff forming the tenors and the majority of the bass voices. In July of that year sixty cadets, seven masters, the Padre and the Medical Officer, enjoyed the Choir and Band outing to Paignton.

Drawing classes were part of the curriculum and the cadets were encouraged to develop their creative talents, as the frequent artistic contributions to illustrate the *Britannia Magazine* testify.

8 Mr H. E. Piggott became Head of Mathematics and the Second Master.

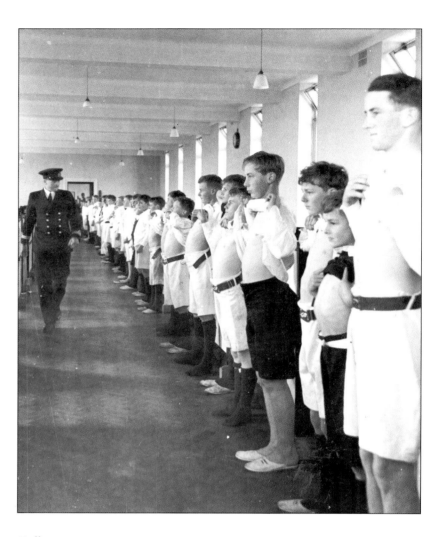

Belly muster.

Photography was also popular, with a darkroom having been available to cadets since the latter days of the old *Britannia*. Their contributions were frequently used to illustrate the *Britannia Magazine*. The study of Natural History had a strong following, supported by the College Field Club, here cadets would take rambles in the countryside and observe the local fauna and flora, birds and in particular their nests. There is no doubt that collecting bird's eggs was a popular hobby at this time, as photographs of nests with eggs frequently appear in the *Britannia Magazine* (one cadet had lost his life in the quest to collect eggs, falling from a cliff, when the *Britannia* was moored at Portland in 1862).

Drama productions have also been a part of College life from the days of the hulks on the river up to the present day and cadets were encouraged to take part in all aspects of the production. Model making too was a hobby enjoyed by young boys. Naturally boats were a particularly popular theme for modelling, with the Britannia Model Boat Club meeting at Sandquay, where they sailed their

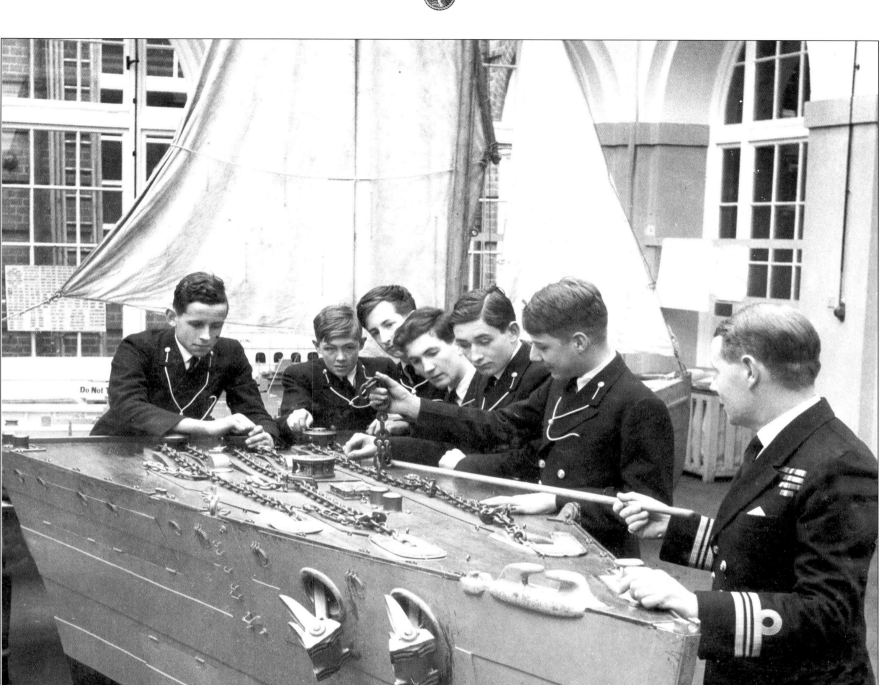

Seamanship instruction utilising the fo'c'sle of HMS Rodney. *This bow model was built by the engineering company of Basset-Lowke Ltd. of Northampton and is fondly remembered by generations of naval officers. It was dismantled in 1997 but the two anchors survive to serve as doorstops.*

'The Old Canteen,' a watercolour appearing in the Britannia Magazine*, by Cadet W. St. J. Ainslie, before it was replaced in 1930.*

craft. In 1917 there had been 150 members of the Britannia Model Boat Club, a not inconsiderable proportion of the College population. One of the more unusual clubs met in the classroom of Mr J. S. Sampson, the History and English Master. He had an interest in medieval weaponry and built models of the types of weapons used to storm and defend great castles. The top edge of the blackboard in his classroom was decorated with castellated battlements resembling a medieval castle. The club would meet in the afternoon, after lessons, and he would demonstrate how these weapons worked by firing projectiles at the battlements. As a special treat at the end of term the cadets would be allowed to operate the miniature weapons themselves.

Sport played a highly significant part in the daily life of the College, recognised as providing not just recreational activity but a means of instilling the qualities of team spirit and leadership, vital for a Naval Officer. [9] The prominence of sport was spelt out very clearly in the guide *How to Become a Naval Officer (Dartmouth)* (1945):

'From the point of view of sport, Dartmouth challenges comparison with any school in the world.

9 See box on College Sport.

There are eighteen acres of playing grounds, devoted to rugger, soccer, cricket and hockey. The College maintains a pack of beagles, started over fifty years ago, and famous throughout the district.

Half-way down to the river are the racquet courts, and on the river itself are the boat houses containing skiffs and gigs. Above the College are a large gymnasium and a swimming-bath, the latter the scene of strenuous water-polo matches. The keenest competition rages between the various Houses as to which can accumulate the greatest number of trophies in their gun-rooms, as every branch of sport, from rugger to cross-country running, including rifle shooting, has a challenge cup for competition ... Last, but not least, we must not forget the canteen, which stands so conveniently among the playing grounds, and beneath whose hospitable roofs vast quantities of delicious food are consumed by a seething mass of cadets straight from the battlefields of sport.

Without the slightest fear of contradiction one may assert that to 99 per cent of the cadets who pass through Dartmouth, the period spent there remains for all times the happiest of memories.'

Officers and Masters in the Common Room in 1941. Among those assembled are the Headmaster Mr. Kempson (standing third from right) and keen photographer Mr John Barlee (second from right).

Within this idyll there could have been the temptation to become complacent. In 1926 HM Inspectorate of Schools observed that 'the staff was tending to become a smooth-running, efficient machine rather than a body of pioneers developing new ideas and a new system.' (Davies & Grove 1980, p.15) This otherwise complementary report also remarked that while great care was taken of weaker students there was little opportunity for the intellectual development of the most able. It was against this background in 1927 that second Headmaster Mr E. W. Kempson took over from Cyril Ashford, who was awarded a knighthood for his services. An engineer, Kempson had taught at Dartmouth before the war as both a Naval Instructor and civilian master, before becoming head of the science department at Rugby School. During the war he had served with the Royal Engineers and won the Military Cross. After the war he had returned to the field of education as an Inspector of

10 His eldest daughter, Rachel became an actress and married the actor Sir Michael Redgrave. The celebrity couple were married in the College Chapel in 1935.

Schools.[10] One of Kempson's first acts, in 1928, was the introduction of 'Alpha classes'. Under this system the ablest students in the eighth term would be chosen to take one subject (not mathematics, but science, modern languages or history and English) at a subsidiary level, allowing more time to be spent on the remaining three. Much of this additional work would involve private study thus affording cadets the opportunity to manage their own time under a slightly more relaxed routine.

By the early 1930s the College was once again coming under outside scrutiny. Against the backdrop of economic depression and continuing disarmament Dartmouth appeared an extravagance with 412 staff to 408 students in 1932. Part of the problem was that a naval career was simply not felt to be an attractive proposition at the time, thus reducing the number of suitable applicants. Those for whom a career in the Navy might appeal were increasingly drawn towards the more flexible arrangements of the Special Entry. There was also mounting concern over the quality of the Dartmouth cadet, particularly when compared to the public school boys of the Special

Entry. As a mark of this concern the captains of ships taking cadets into the fleet were asked to report back to Dartmouth on their progress (BRNC Archive). The results were mixed. One captain observed:

'The main difference between the Dartmouth and the Special Entry officer is the narrowness of outlook of the former; this is shown in their conversation and lack of knowledge on matters outside the Service. The main topics of conversation on Officers' messes are 'shop' and 'games.'… The Public School man is wider read and more knowledgeable about the least detraction to his job.

The Dartmouth system tends to create officers of the deserving, unimaginative type who take matters as they find them. The Late Entry on the other hand produces officers who lead their men and are more inclined to strike out on a line of their own.'

The captain of HMS *Valiant* was more sympathetic:

'I think there is very little wrong with the modern Naval Cadet as he leaves Dartmouth. He is bound to suffer in comparison with the Public School boy when each joins his first ship because the Dartmouth boy is one to one and a half years younger.

The world rarely makes allowances; people are judged at their face value, and the Public School boy, with his greater age and more self-assurance, gets away with it every time.'

Part of the problem was perceived to be the independence and responsibility that was afforded to the public school boy in his sixth form, for which there was no equivalent at Dartmouth. Consequently when Admiral Dunbar-Nasmith VC, Captain of the College 1926-29, became Second Sea Lord in 1936 he determined to introduce a house system at Dartmouth. Following a whistle-stop tour of seven public schools undertaken by Captain Dalrymple-Hamilton and having taken advice from various headmasters, the House system was introduced in 1937. Under this new organisation there were to be five houses, – Blake, Exmouth, Grenville, Hawke and St.Vincent, plus a separate 'Drake' house for cadets in their first two terms. By replacing the term system with that of houses, cadets were able to mix with boys of different ages and develop a sense of loyalty and attachment to a house that would not change at the end of every term. The system also allowed for increased responsibility to be devolved to senior cadets as both cadet and house captains. The

problem of staff turnover remained, with house officers having to move on after two or three years but it now became possible to affiliate masters to a specific house to act as tutors and assist with the organisation of games. Indeed inter-house sports became more competitive as in term competitions the advantage had usually rested with the more senior term. Despite some initial concerns about laxity of discipline the house system was to prove most successful and continued until the end of the thirteen-year-old entry after the Second World War.

Meanwhile, in the outside world, international relations continued to deteriorate. In September 1938, as the leaders of Britain, France, Germany and Italy met at Munich, sandbags were filled by cadets and placed around the College. In May 1939 Special Entry cadets arrived at Dartmouth for the first time. Their training cruiser HMS *Frobisher* was being refitted for active service, so instead of going to sea the eighteen-year-olds were accommodated in the ship's company barracks block (now Beatty). Finally war was declared on 3rd September 1939. The initial impact of the war upon the College was minimal, until 18th September 1942 when the College was bombed and rendered unfit to continue as a place of education. Despite the subsequent evacuation to Eaton Hall in Cheshire the routine of the College was to remain unchanged throughout the rest of the conflict.[11]

That the scheme fought for by Fisher and Selborne lasted for almost half a century is a mark of the forethought that had contributed to a unique system of naval education. Arguably many of its original objectives failed to transpire; engineers were to remain at a disadvantage and after 1921 were not generally to receive a Dartmouth education, while an increasing number of officers of all branches were to enter the service via the Special Entry at the age of eighteen, too old to be properly moulded for life at sea. Nevertheless Dartmouth had been successfully established as a public school for naval officers, in which it was possible to combine the staff and curriculum for what was recognised as a good general education with the unique professional training the Navy required. However, as the College returned to Dartmouth in September 1946 few could have anticipated the changes that were about to be wrought. The world and Britain's place in it had changed and so would Dartmouth.

11 See Chapter 5 The College at War.

CHAPTER 4

The Royal College

The Verge carried by the usher (left of photograph) ahead of Her Majesty Queen Elizabeth as she inspects the Guard at Lord High Admiral's Divisions in 1972.

T he Royal connection with the British Navy is centuries old. The Royal Family's association with Dartmouth, as frequent visitors, cadets and indeed the parents, grandparents, and brothers and sisters of cadets dates back to the College's earliest years.

To prescribe a date to the origins of the modern Royal Navy would be to invoke controversy, although the Restoration Navy of 1660 is often accepted as such. The Senior Gunroom panelling of the College, however, chooses a much earlier date at which to start the connection of King and Navy. Elaborately carved in the upper parts of the panelling are commemorated famous naval engagements and the personalities associated with them. Prominently over the entrance door the carved letters covered with gold-leaf, proclaim 'ALFRED: THE DANES: 897'. This was only a minor encounter but demonstrated the use of ships by a King for the defence of our shores and makes Alfred the first English monarch to recognise the importance of sea power to an island nation. Thus Alfred is often regarded as the 'Father of the Navy'. However, his victory over the Danes as commemorated in the Senior Gun Room was not his first seagoing engagement, an action in 875 has that distinction (Rodger 1997, p.10). Moreover, the *Anglo-Saxon Chronicles* record the date of the engagement as 896 (ibid. p.16). The controversy over the precise date of the engagement might in fact be due to the English civil calendar dating the start of the New Year from Lady Day (25 March) (see Rodger page xix). Nevertheless, the choice of this action and this date probably has as much to do with the Diamond Jubilee of Queen Victoria in 1897 as it does with historical accuracy and thus emphasises the thousand-year association of the Monarch and the Navy. Hence the royal connection can be said to be well in excess of a thousand years.

The Princes Albert Victor and George in their cadet uniforms. These official photographs were taken, as they were about to join HMS Britannia *in 1877.*

Edward III became known as 'The King of the Seas' after his bowmen gained victory at the battle of Sluys in 1340, another battle commemorated in the carved panelling of the Senior Gunroom.

It was under Henry VIII that a true navy was born, and he is often referred to as 'The Father of the English Navy' but it was his daughter Elizabeth I, who recognised the potential of a maritime fleet. Francis Drake was appointed as Rear Admiral and he played a major role in the defence of our shores by repelling the Spanish Armada. It was men such as Frobisher, Grenville, Hawkins, Howard and Raleigh, who gained notoriety at this time, the first two giving their names to 'Terms' at the College.

It was during the English Civil War that a number of generals established some command of the sea and such men as Robert Blake and George Monck were recognised as both seamen and leaders. The name of Blake for many years was one of the College Divisions and Monck is another name celebrated in the Senior Gunroom panelling. Admiral Blake had gained a reputation in the war against the Dutch and this in turn led to a fleet being raised and sent to Holland under Monck to bring back Charles II to the throne of England. It was with the restoration of Charles II that the Navy was truly established, indeed it was Charles who granted the Royal prefix in 1660. The Royal Navy was now truly born.

The Naval Discipline Act of 1661 founded the Royal Navy by permanent Statute. The act bore the following in its preamble: 'His Majesty's Navies, ships of War, and forces by Sea, wherein under the good Providence and Protection of God, the Wealth, Safety and Strength of his Kingdom is so much concerned.' This view was first expressed by the Commons in 1415 as '*La dit Naveye est la griendre substance du bein, profit et prosperitee du vostre dit Rioalme*' and is misquoted rather elegantly, carved in Portland stone, on the front of the College as:

IT. IS: ON. THE: NAVY UNDER: THE: GOOD:
PROVIDENCE OF: GOD: THAT. OUR WEALTH:
PROSPERITY: AND PEACE: DEPEND

Even though the Act received minor amendments in 1749 and 1816 to '…wealth, safety and strength of the Kingdom chiefly depend' the carving on the College front is still not as originally quoted and was probably shortened and altered to fit the space available.

The Lord High Admiral

When the High Court of Admiralty was formed early in the fifteenth century, The Earl of Dorset was placed at its head with the title Admiral of England, Ireland and Aquitaine in 1408 (Rodger 1997, p.149). Subsequent heads of the Court were referred to as Great Admiral or Lord Admiral, and in 1547 Baron Seymour of Sudeley was appointed Lord High Admiral. In the reign of Henry VIII they took command of the fleet at sea, and through the Navy Board, also took charge of naval administration. The judicial functions finally passed to

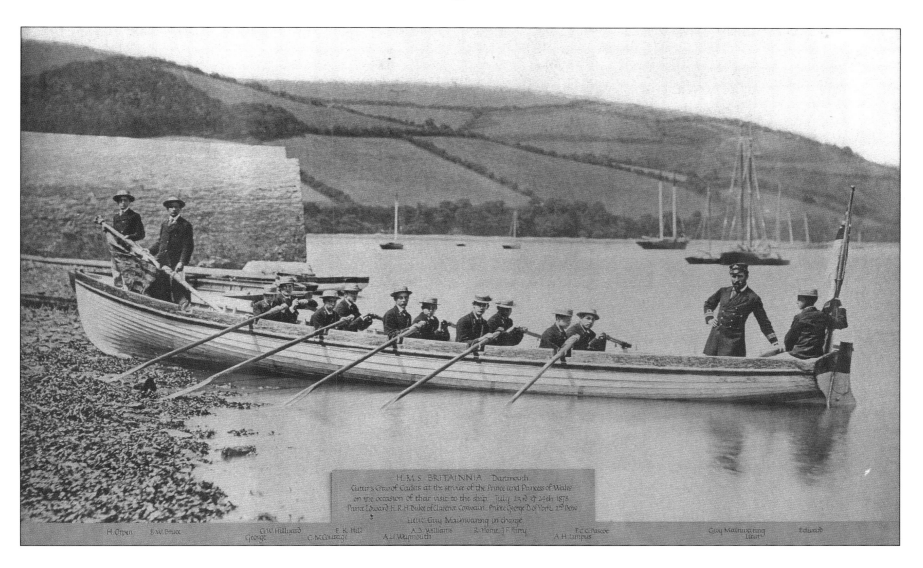

A College cutter at the service of the Prince and Princess of Wales when they visited HMS Britannia *on 23rd and 24th July 1878. Prince George is the second bow oar, nearest to the camera. Prince Edward (Albert Victor) is the coxswain.*

the High Court of Justice in 1875. During the years from 1628 to 1964 the office was vested in committees, commissions or boards.

The post of Lord High Admiral has been held by James, Duke of York (later King James II) from 1660 to 1673; King Charles II (1685); King James II (1685); Prince George of Denmark (Consort of Queen Anne) from 1702 – 1708; and from 1827 – 1828 William, Duke of Clarence (later King William IV).

In 1964 when the Admiralty, along with the War Office and Air Ministry combined to form the Ministry of Defence, the Admiralty became the Admiralty Board of the Defence Council and Her Majesty Queen Elizabeth II graciously consented to assume the title of Lord High Admiral.

In 1970 Her Majesty approved Admiral of the Fleet Earl Mountbatten of Burma's proposal that each year one of the passing

out parades at the Britannia Royal Naval College should be called the Lord High Admiral's Divisions. In addition the salute at these Divisions should be taken by Her Majesty or by her personal representative, this nearly always a member of the Royal Family.

The Royal Verge or Wand

The Verge or Wand was made in 1662 for James, Duke of York, as a symbol of the authority and jurisdiction of the Lord High Admiral. It is carried by the usher ahead of the Lord High Admiral or her representative at Lord High Admiral's Divisions. The head is of solid silver and was kept on board the Royal Yacht *Britannia*. When the Royal Yacht was decommissioned it was given to the College and can still be seen in a case near the front entrance.

The Royal Princes Edward (Albert Victor) and George on board
HMS Britannia. *The photograph is dated 3rd March 1878 and signed by*
both Princes. It is framed with wood taken from the old Britannia *when she*
was broken up in 1916. The photograph is inscribed on the back 'Sprat' and
'Herring'. Sprat referring to Prince George and Herring, Prince Edward.

Royal Cadets

The Princes Albert Victor and George

It had long been a tradition for the second son of the monarch or heir apparent to join the Royal Navy. This had been so in the case of Queen Victoria's second son, Alfred Duke of Edinburgh, who had been a cadet on board HMS *Illustrious* and *Britannia*, at Portsmouth. It was therefore natural that Prince George, the second son of Prince Edward the Prince of Wales (later Edward VII) should follow a career in the Navy. By the time Prince George was twelve years old (one of the youngest cadets to ever join the ship) the route of entry for a naval cadet began on board the training ship HMS *Britannia*, moored in the River Dart.

However, a problem existed in sending Prince George away to Dartmouth. His elder brother, Albert Victor (also known as Prince Edward or 'Eddy') the Duke of Clarence, was a rather backward child who relied heavily upon his younger brother for support. The boys' tutor, Canon Dalton, therefore suggested that both Princes should join *Britannia*, thus affording Albert Victor the opportunity to develop 'those habits of promptitude and method, of manliness and self-reliance, in which he is somewhat deficient.' (Rose 1983, p.6.) The Prince of Wales agreed that the education and discipline they would receive in the Navy would prove invaluable and approved of the suggestion. The Queen, however, while agreeing that George should make the Navy his career, had reservations about the suitability of the lifestyle for a future monarch: 'The very rough sort of life to which boys are exposed on board ship is the very thing not calculated to make a refined and amiable prince.' (Hampshire 1971, p.116.) Moreover, she expressed her concern that a 'nautical education' might 'engender and encourage national prejudices and make them think that their own Country is superior to any other.' (Rose 1983, p.7.) The First Lord of the Admiralty and the Prime Minister, Mr Disraeli, who advised the Queen against the idea, shared her concerns.

Finally the Queen acquiesced on the condition that Canon Dalton accompany the Princes on board the ship. Subsequently, the boys sat the entrance exam for the Royal Naval College, which included arithmetic, algebra, geometry, diction, reading English 'intelligently', French translation, the Scriptures, geography and English history, in April 1877, achieving satisfactory results. In October of that year the Prince of Wales, wearing the full dress uniform of a captain in the Royal Naval Reserve, accompanied his sons and their tutor on board *Britannia*. They were to be treated as any other cadet on the ship, their only privilege being to sling their hammocks in a private cabin on the poop deck, above the captain's. In common with many of the cadets they were given their own nicknames, 'Sprat' and 'Herring', as befitting the sons of the Prince of W(h)ales. They messed with all their classmates and were subject to the same restrictions, including the ban on food on board and the limit of one shilling a week pocket money, as George V was later to recount to his librarian, Sir Owen Moreshead:

'It never did me any good to be a Prince, I can tell you, and many was the time I wished I hadn't been. It was a pretty tough place and, so far from making any allowances for our disadvantages, the other boys made a point of taking it out on us on the grounds that they'd never be able to do it later on . . . Then we had a sort of tuck-shop on land, up the steep hill; only we weren't allowed to bring any eatables into the ship, and they used to search you as you came aboard. Well the big boys used to fag me to bring them back a whole lot of stuff – and I was always found out and got into trouble in addition to having the stuff confiscated . . . we were only given a shilling a week pocket money, so it meant a lot to me I can tell you.' (Rose 1983, p.7.)

George seemed to suffer particularly from financial hardships, his pleas to his Grandmother to send him a sovereign to tide him over meeting with a kindly but firm refusal on the basis that it would be inappropriate to break the restrictions placed upon all the cadets. Fortunately not all cadets' families were so inflexible, and on recounting his story to a wealthy friend, George was offered three pounds for the Queen's letter, which he accepted.

Being directly in line for the throne it was recognised that Albert Victor would not be making the Navy his career, a point not missed

Official photograph of Prince George while he was a cadet on Britannia.

A drawing by Prince Edward, Duke of Clarence, recently discovered in the College archive. Drawing and art classes were held on board Britannia, *after all this was a school and the normal school subjects were taught in addition to seamanship etc. The drawing shows some grasp of both perspective and light and shade and such skills would be useful to a naval officer later in his career when as a Midshipman he would need to be able to illustrate his 'Journal'.*

by his younger brother who allegedly advised his instructors to focus their attention upon him. Indeed while the Duke of Clarence remained distant and lethargic, George fitted into the naval lifestyle with ease. He took his training seriously, dutifully performing the most lowly of tasks, such as scrubbing the deck, thoroughly and with care. He was skilful in seamanship and handling boats and was also good at mathematics. His sense of humour also suited life aboard *Britannia*, entering into the spirit of all the pranks, while his brother chose to take no notice. Finally, in 1879, the two princes passed out of *Britannia* to join their first sea-going ship, HMS *Bacchante*. Prince George was to see service for a total of almost twenty-two years, serving in a number of battleships before taking command of a torpedo boat in 1889. He subsequently commanded the gunboat HMS *Thrush* and (as a Captain) the cruisers *Melampus* and *Crescent*. However, in January 1892 Victor Albert, who had suffered from ill health throughout his life, died leaving George as his father's successor to the throne.

The Princes Albert Victor and George on board Britannia, *c.1878.*

The Princes Edward and Albert

As Prince of Wales, George recognised that his naval education had not perhaps been the most appropriate preparation for a future monarch, and that an understanding of politics, international affairs, history and languages would have been more valuable than the practicalities of seamanship and navigation. Nevertheless, when it was suggested by their tutor, Henry Hansell, that his sons Edward and Albert might benefit from attending prep school his reply was emphatic: 'My brother and I never went to prep school, the Navy will teach them all they need to know.' (Hampshire 1971, p.146.) So it was that the next generation of royal princes entered the Royal Navy.

By 1907, when Prince Edward was twelve years old, the *Britannia* on which his father and uncle had received their education had been replaced by the shore based College. However, before he could enter Dartmouth, the naval cadet of the twentieth century had first to spend two years at the Royal Naval College Osborne, built around the stables of the late Queen Victoria's residence. Edward arrived at Osborne in May 1907, with his father on board the Admiralty yacht, *Enchantress*, to join the Exmouth Term. In common with all the other new cadets, Edward had undergone both oral and written examinations before joining. He did well in the oral exam, in which one of the questions was whether he was afraid of the dark, but did rather less well in the written part, failing to achieve the minimum mark required by five points. He was not, however, the only boy to have done so and still make it on to the College. Indeed, the Prince of Wales was insistent that his son should be treated the same as any other cadet, a decree that naval outfitter Mr Gieve found difficult to accept, replacing Prince Edward's standard issue rough blue rug for one of fine quality cashmere. His fellow cadets, however, had rather less difficulty in treating him as one of their own, subjecting him to the same initiation ordeals and mild bullying that everyone incurred. On one occasion classmates used a classroom window to re-enact the beheading of Charles I and on another poured red ink over his head. The latter incident caused Edward to miss evening quarters rather than give away his persecutors, a move that earned him three days' extra drill. He was also christened with the obligatory nickname, in this case 'Sardines', a not exactly original reference to his father's royal title.

Both Edward and his younger brother joined Osborne at a distinct disadvantage, not merely because of their royal status. Until the age of twelve or thirteen neither had experienced being taught in a classroom of more than three pupils, by a tutor whose teaching failed to prepare them fully for the Naval College's curriculum. They had not spent much time in the company of children their own age, slept in a dormitory or been away from home. In contrast, their peers at Osborne and Dartmouth would have had up to seven years at prep school to get used to such conditions. Nevertheless, by the end of his final term at Osborne Edward had become a popular if not brilliant student. The next step was Dartmouth.

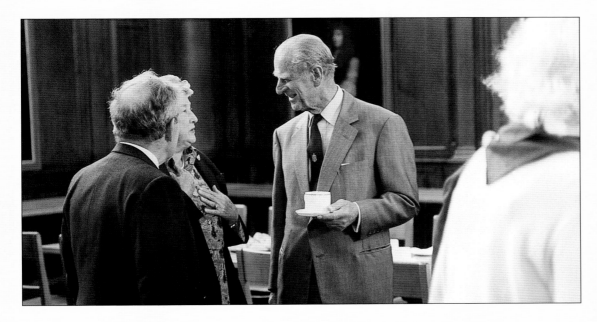

Prince Philip takes tea with his former class-mates and their wives in July 1999.

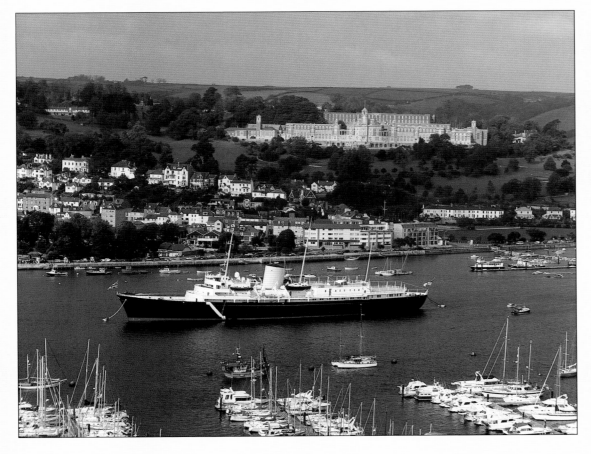

HMY *Britannia* during a visit to Dartmouth in 1992.

Top: Prince Andrew, shortly after passing out from Dartmouth as a Midshipman, signs the visitors' book, a tradition for all Royal visitors.

Middle: Prince Charles examines his class photograph, with Commodore Roy Clare during an informal visit in 1999.

Bottom: Goodbye: HM The Queen waves to the assembled crowds as she leaves on the Royal Barge in July 1972. Prince Philip salutes while Lord Louis Mountbatten, Princess Anne and a young Prince Andrew are all safely aboard for their short journey to HMY *Britannia*.

the water of Dartmouth. His next step as a cadet should have been a six-month training cruise in one of the cruisers attached to the College, HMS *Cumberland* or *Cornwall*. Unfortunately, with the coronation due to take place on 22nd June 1911, he was unable to join his classmates, being instead promoted to the rank of midshipman by his father on the eve of the coronation and later joining the battleship *Hindustan*. Nevertheless Dartmouth seemed to have made a good impression on the Royal Family, the King noting, 'I certainly think the College is the best school in England.' A sentiment which was apparently shared by Prince Edward, who following a visit to Winchester School, wrote to his father; 'It is amusing to see the difference between an ordinary school and Dartmouth . . . Their life is not half as strenuous as it is at Dartmouth and we were more contented. There can be no better education than a naval one.' (Ziegler, 1990, p.28.)

For Prince Albert, though, his naval education still had a long way to go. Albert had joined Osborne as a member of the Grenville Term in January 1909. It was Edward's final term there and he was tasked by his father to look after his younger brother, to 'put him up to the ropes' and make sure that he worked hard. (Zeigler 1990, p.22.) This task was not easy as boys from different Terms were not supposed to mix with each other, causing the royal brothers to meet clandestinely at the top of the playing fields. Albert inevitably suffered from comparison with his brother, suffering as he did from the extra disadvantages of being shy and nervous. Mr Watt, Albert's Osborne tutor, wrote: 'One could wish that he had more of Prince Edward's keenness and application.' While a contemporary of the two princes at Osborne and Dartmouth commented that it was: 'like comparing an ugly duckling with a cock pheasant.' (Bradford 1989, p.63.) His stammer contributed to the bullying of other cadets while his determination to hide it baffled and irritated his masters who thought him either stupid or very shy. As he was later to confide to a friend, he chose to remain silent in maths classes to avoid pronouncing the letter 'f' in 'fraction'. Fortunately his father seemed to appreciate his problem, writing to the brothers' old tutor, Hansell: 'Watt thinks Bertie shy in class. I expect it is his dislike of showing his hesitating speech that prevents him from answering.' (Bradford 1989, p.56.) One senior staff officer, who knew them both, remarked that he considered 'the younger will outstrip the elder.' (Hampshire 1971, p.159.)

Albert was not good at rugby or cricket but had an aptitude for athletics, winning him the appreciation and respect of his peers. Academically, however, he struggled, regularly occupying the lower few places in end of term results. Indeed there was real concern that Albert would not make the grade to move up to Dartmouth, prompting the Prince of Wales to write sternly to his son:

'I am sorry to say that the last reports from Mr Watt with regard to your work are not at all satisfactory, he says you don't seem to take your work seriously, nor do you appear to be very keen about it. My dear boy this will not do, if you go on like this you will be at the bottom of your Term, you are now 71st and you won't pass your examination and very probably will be warned this term if you don't take care . . . everything rests with you and you are quite intelligent and can do very well if you like. I trust that you will take to heart what I have written and that the next report will be a good one and the others to come until the end of term.' (Wheeler-Bennett, 1958, p.45 – 46.)

Prince Albert seemed to take his father's warning to heart, with noted improvement in his powers of concentration and willingness to use them, causing Mr Watt to report that 'His Royal Highness has done better and more consistent work than he has done in any previous term.' (Ibid. p.46 – 47.) However, as the final examinations approached so did the Christmas holidays and in the excitement Albert, in Mr Watt's words, seemed to go 'a mucker', finishing sixty-eighth out of sixty-eight.

Nevertheless, in January 1911 Albert joined his elder brother at Dartmouth, only to find himself one month later laid up by the latest epidemic of measles and mumps. This was followed by a period of sick-leave and recuperation in Newquay, Cornwall. He returned to Dartmouth two days before the end of term, having spent no more than a total of four weeks of his first term at the College. Albert's second term was also disrupted, this time by his father's coronation on 22nd June, an occasion for which he wore his Naval Cadet's uniform.

The regime at Dartmouth expected more maturity from its cadets than Osborne, allowing greater responsibilities and freedoms. Albert's new term officer, Lieutenant Henry Spencer Cooper, encouraged the young prince to pursue cross-country running, riding and to follow the Britannia Beagles. He also became good at tennis and sailing, seizing the opportunity to take the College boats up the River Dart to Totnes and Dittisham to enjoy tea with the locals. Sports were not the only extra-curricular activity in which Albert participated. On one occasion he was caught along with sixteen other cadets letting off illicit fireworks on Guy Fawkes' Night. As punishment for this misdemeanour he received 'six of the best', although he always maintained an injustice had occurred as the cane had broken after four strokes. Such escapades or 'skylarking' were not unusual but one such episode was to have more impact than the average prank. In February 1912, the King and Queen returned home from the great Coronation Durbar in India, planning to visit the Naval College in March. But the Britain to which they had returned was in the grip of industrial unrest and anti-establishment protest. A rumour started to circulate around Dartmouth that some of the senior cadets planned to mark the forthcoming royal visit by painting the newly installed statue of the King with red paint. The Captain of the College took the rumour seriously, ordering a twenty-four hour watch to be posted on the statue. Some of the civilian staff required to form the guard threatened to strike and were subsequently sacked. In a letter to his parents Prince

R. T. BOWER, P. F. P. WOOD, V. G. SNOW, H. B. DEEDES, H. T. DAWSON, W. B. PRICE, C. V. POWEL, PRINCE EDWARD, M. J. BETHELL.

UT. BEASLEY, MR. MCKEAN, MR ARKWRIGHT, J. M. MANSFIELD, ENG.-LIEUT. FOSTER, H. R. K. BAMBER, MR. BRYANT, G. H. WARNER, Y. H. F. G. WELLS, J. M. P. ROWLANDSON, MR. ANSTIE, MR. PIGGOTT, G. R. COUSINS

H. S. BARKER, W. S. R. KING-HALL, LIEUT. NICHOLSON, MR. HOPE, C. JENKIN, DR. PICK, D. WAINWRIGHT, MR. MEGSON, J. L. DAVIES, MR. MERCER, LIEUT. FORD.

H.M.S. PINAFORE, CHRISTMAS 1909.

The College production of 'HMS Pinafore', staged at Christmas 1909. Prince Edward played the First Lord's sister and can be seen standing at the back, second from the right. The photograph is taken at the rear of O block, or what is now the lower library.

WAR SERVICES.

(Giving full particulars of campaigns, engagements, wounds, mentions in despatches, medals, awards, decorations, etc.)

I served in the Grand Fleet in August 1914 in the "Collingwood". Again from February 1915 to August 1915. Again from May 1916 to August 1916 and from May 1917 to August 1917 in the "Malaya". In February 1918 I was attached to the R.N.A.S. at Cranwell Lines, and remained on there in the R.A.F. till August when I was appointed to the R.A.F. Cadet Brigade Hastings and subsequently transferred to Shorncliffe when the Brigade moved in September.

I was present at the Battle of Jutland on May 31st 1916.

I was mentioned in despatches

Knight of the Garter
Queen Victoria's Diamond Jubilee Medal
King Edward's Coronation Medal
King George's Coronation Medal
Order of the White Eagle (I Class) Serbian.
Order of St. Vladimir (IV class) Russian.

I hereby certify that I am satisfied of the general correctness of all the above particulars as to qualifications, services, etc., set out on pages 2, 3 and 4.

.... Commanding Officer.

Station .... Regiment.

1

Army Form B. 199.

RECORD OF SERVICES.

of Captain H.R.H. Prince Albert

(Rank, Christian Names and Surname in full, printed).

Regiment Royal Navy (attached Royal Air Force)
Lieutenant

PERSONAL PARTICULARS.

1. Date and Place of Birth ...
(If promoted from the ranks, age as given on attestation and date of attestation should be stated in lieu of date of birth.)
York Cottage Sandringham Norfolk December 14th 1895.

2. Religious persuasion ...
Church of England

3. Where educated, specifying Schools or University ...
Royal Naval College Osborne " " " Dartmouth.

4. Date of first Commission ...
May 15th 1916.

5. Height ...
5 ft. 9 ½ inches

6. Married or Single ...
Single

7. If married, date of marriage ...
—

8. Name and Address of next of kin (stating relationship), guardian or agent for reference in case of emergency ...
His Majesty The King Buckingham Palace London S.W.

also

A second name (as an alternative) ...
Her Majesty The Queen

I do hereby certify that to the best of my knowledge and belief this statement of personal particulars is in all respects correct and true.

Albert .... Signature of Officer.

Place Dibgate Camp Shorncliffe Captain .... Rank.

Date October 3rd 1918 Royal Air Force .... Regiment.

(A9113) Wt. W9350/P120 90,000 10/17 D. D. & L. Sch. 29. Gen. No. 1357

The Record of War Service of Prince Albert, later King George VI dated 3rd October 1918, is on Army Form B99 and is in the King's own handwriting.

Albert innocently informed them of the episode:

'Papa's statue has been placed at the end of the Quarterdeck today with Grandpapa's picture on the right of it. It looks very well indeed. Have you seen the small paragraph in today's Daily Graphic on page nine. It is headed "The Statue and the Strike". It is supposed that some cadets were going to paint it, so the cadets' servants were told to watch it at night, to prevent anyone from doing so.' (Wheeler-Bennett 1958, p.55.)

In the end the visit had to be cancelled due to a five-week long coal strike. Albert failed to persuade his father to grant an extra week's leave as compensation.

In his last term at Dartmouth Albert was given the opportunity to accompany his father on board the Royal Yacht, *Victoria and Albert*, to witness the review of the Fleet off Weymouth, in May 1912. It was during this excursion that the future king met his future prime minister, Winston Churchill, who was then First Lord of the Admiralty.

Overall, Dartmouth seemed to have a positive impact upon Prince Albert. He was never to excel academically but to finish sixty-first out of sixty-seven could be seen as a relative improvement, leading Captain Evan-Thomas to conclude, 'I think he will do'. (Wheeler-Bennett 1958, p.58.) In terms of personal development Albert had clearly matured and achieved general popularity among fellow cadets, masters, staff officers and civilian workers. He was respected for his persistence, generosity, loyalty and sense of humour, but most of all because he never talked 'up' or 'down' to anyone. All this stood him in great stead for the next part of his training on board HMS *Cumberland*, which would lead to his promotion to the rank of midshipman and a career in the Royal Navy. He would next visit Dartmouth on the eve of the Second World War, accompanied by his wife and two daughters.

The last of King George's children to be educated by the Navy, was Prince George, the Duke of Kent. By the time he joined Osborne in September 1916 the First World War was already well underway. The Royal Navy was contemplating the outcome of the Battle of Jutland that had taken place earlier that year and at which Prince Albert had been present, serving on board HMS *Collingwood*. For George the war meant a foreshortening of his education, spending just three, instead of the usual six terms at Osborne before joining Dartmouth in September 1917. By way of compensation he was to spend, along with his classmates, seven terms at Dartmouth but the overall experience was to prove an unhappy one. Temperamentally unsuited to naval life George hated his time at Dartmouth and indeed was to spend most of his career pleading to be allowed to leave the Navy. This was reflected in his performance at the College, where he passed out eighty-fifth out of eighty-six. Prince George finally left the Royal Navy in 1934 but he was to find himself back in uniform at the outbreak of World War Two. Tragically on the 25th August 1942 the plane in which he was flying

Prince Albert, the future King George VI, at the front door of the College in 1911.

HOBSON	E. A.	KEENE	A. N. R.	LUKE		J. C.
HOFFMAN	A. A.	KELLETT	W. B.	LOVATT		R. S.
HOLBROOK	G. N.	KELSEY	V. H.			
HOLLAND	K. T.	KEMP	N. McI.	McCLINTOCK		J. L. E.
HOLLOWAY	D. R.	KENNAWAY	C. S. H.	McCULLOCH		A. C.
HOOPER	B. R.	KENNEDY	M. H. McL.	MACDERMOTT		A.
HOPE	C. W.	KENNEDY	R.	MACDONNELL		L. W. A.
HORNELL	D. A. H.	H.R.H. DUKE of KENT	G. E. A. E.	MACHIN		J. L.
HOSKIN	M. C.	KERR	R.	MACHIN		M. N.
HOTHAM	C. E.	KETTLE	L. H.	MACK		P. J.
HOUSTON	D. A.	KINDER	R.	MACKENDRICK		D. W.
HOWARD	H. G. P.	KINDERSLEY	A. T. J.	MACKINNON		A. H. I.
HOWDEN	I. C.	KING	H. V.	MACKINNON		D. S.
HUDDART	G. P.	KING–CHURCH	J. B.	MACLEISH		A. A. F.
HUDDART	J. S.	KIPLING	R. F.	MACPHERSON		M. H.
HULBERT	W. B.	KNOWLES	A.	MAINPRICE		W. J.
HUMPHREYS	P. N.	KNOWLES	H. G.	MANDEVILLE		G. F.
HUNT	H. G.	KNOWLING	R. G. K.	MANSELL		J. F.
HUNT	J. P.	KNOX	W. N. R.	MANSELL		J. O.
HUNT	M. H.			MANWARING		A. H.

HRH Prince George outside the main entrance of the College in 1920.
In common with all former cadets who lost their life during the Second
World, the Duke of Kent's name is recorded on the College war memorial.

crashed, killing all on board. Having lost his life in the service of his country, the Duke of Kent's name was added to the College war memorial alongside those of fellow former cadets.

Prince Louis of Battenberg

Prince Louis joined the Royal Naval College Osborne as a member of the Exmouth Term in May 1913. He had done well in his entrance exam, passing fifteenth out of eighty-three, doing best in English and German and worst in arithmetic. He entered the College at potentially a double disadvantage, being not only royal, but the son of the First Sea Lord, the Marquis of Milford Haven. His royal status was reflected in the particularly small writing on the brass plaque on his sea chest, so as to accommodate the title 'Serene Highness'. In common with all the other royal cadets 'Dickie' was subjected to the same bullying as the other boys. On joining his 'ordeal' was to climb the flagstaff and sing 'A Life on the Ocean Wave'. On the whole, however, Prince Louis was able to stand his own against the bullies, even challenging an older boy to a fight and winning. Usually this would have been considered a cardinal sin but his opponent was unpopular with the rest of the College, henceforth Louis was something of a hero amongst his classmates. Nor was the son of the most senior Naval Officer in the country exempt from punishment, on one occasion he was rapped so hard over the knuckles with a steel ruler for giggling in bed that he still bore the mark a week later.

In August 1914 war broke out between Britain and Germany. Louis's father, having been born a German, soon found himself victim of the anti-German sentiment that not unnaturally swept the country, finally being forced to resign in October. Back at Osborne Louis found himself ostracised for a short time but this never really amounted to persecution.

Prince Louis arrived at Dartmouth in January 1915, he wrote to his mother giving his first impressions of the Senior College:

'This is an enormous place, almost like a palace. We are all quite lost in it, and as we are apparently not going to be shown round, we will have to find out things for ourselves . . .
The Captain gave us a speech on the quarterdeck after prayers, and then we had to turn in. I was about half-way down my rank, and when we got outside it was literally a race, in which I gained to be about 6th. I then just had time to run off the rusty water in the tap, fill my mug, give one scrub with my brush, and fly back through the passages, nearly lost . . . I went to sleep shortly after 10. In the morning I woke up with the first notes of the old reveille in my ears. I was out of bed with my pyjamas off and my towel on just as the bugle ceased. I then simply flew for the bathroom and was second to get into the plunge. The plunge is not sunk into the ground like the Osborne ones are, but stands up and has only about 2'6" of water in, so I kind of slid in with my mouth open. Alas, I swallowed a mouthful

before I realised it was salt water. Then I hurried off to wash, once more raced up to the dormitory, where I dressed as fast as I could and yet I was only just out within 3 seconds of the time the Cadet Captain gave us. We then had cocoa at about 5 minutes past 7, and then dashed off in the vain hope of finding the right classroom.' (Ziegler 1985, p.37.)

Good academically, Prince Louis was less accomplished when it came to sport, not helped on one occasion when his shorts fell down during a hundred yard race! Some of his letters home hinted of homosexuality being practised among a proportion of the cadets, as he wrote to his mother: 'Some people in the other dormitory have even begun to do filthy things, I have heard.' But Louis himself was far more interested in Admiral Palmer's daughter, Rosamond.

The war was never very far away. In August 1914, the College had received a telegram from the Admiralty, ordering mobilisation, leading to all the cadets being sent to sea ahead of completing their training. There were constant fears that the College would come under attack. During Louis's first term instructions to evacuate were given when it was thought German armed trawlers were nearby and might fire on the College. The incident proved to be a false alarm but from then on Mountbatten kept his greatcoat at the ready and a bag of warm clothes under his bed should it be necessary to leave in a hurry. Then in September 1915, after being at Dartmouth for less than a year, Louis wrote excitedly to his mother: '. . . we are going to sea in January. This has far surpassed my faintest hopes.' (Zeigler 1985, p.39.) However, he was later to be disappointed when the Exmouth Term's departure was postponed until April. Worse was to come though when it was announced that Louis was one of the seventy-two cadets to be sent to the Royal Naval Engineering College at Keyham, Devonport; as Lord Louis was to reflect in the *Britannia Magazine* (July 1965, p.7), 'to our intense indignation we missed the Battle of Jutland by six weeks.' He passed out of Dartmouth eighteenth in his class and subsequently went on to pass out top of his class at Keyham, to commence a naval career which would lead to his appointment as First Sea Lord, making him and his father the only father and son to both hold the post.

Right: The full dress naval uniform of King George VI. It was presented to the College in 1953 by HM Queen Elizabeth and Queen Elizabeth the Queen Mother: "in memory of His late Majesty and of his career in and his devotion for the Royal Navy" (letter dated 5th February 1953 from the Private Secretary to the Queen). The uniform consists of the full dress coat in rank of Admiral of the Fleet, full dress trousers, cocked hat, epaulettes, full dress belt and shoes. In July 1959, Field Marshal Viscount Montgomery of Alamein, KG, visited the College to take the salute at the Passing Out Parade; he forgot to bring his Garter star and so borrowed the one from the King's uniform.

FULL DRESS UNIFORM WORN BY HIS LATE MAJESTY KING GEORGE VI. PRESENTED TO THE ROYAL NAVAL COLLEGE DARTMOUTH BY HER MAJESTY QUEEN ELIZABETH II. AND

The Royal Marine Band

While the origins of the Royal Marine Band Service can be traced back just over a century, (they celebrated their centenary in 2003), Dartmouth has only hosted its own for just under fifty years. Prior to that the Voluntary College Band, formed when the College opened, provided all the music. This band consisted of cadets, civilian staff and officers and it served the College well for fifty years, playing for parades, ballroom dancing lessons and other functions.

It was in July 1903 that the Royal Naval Band marched into the newly formed Royal Naval School of Music at Eastney. The Royal Naval Bandsmen became Royal Marines and they took responsibility for the provision of music for the Royal Navy. However, their arrival at Dartmouth was not until the beginning of 1956 when the Band of HMS Triumph, the ship that had been used for many years as an RN Officer Cadet training ship, marched into the College to assume their new title of the Band of HM Royal Marines Britannia Royal Naval College.

The latter half of the twentieth century had seen huge reductions in the number of ships and of shore establishments and a consequent reduction in the number of bands. The last two ships to retain a band were HMS Ark Royal, which decommissioned in 1978 and HMY Britannia, decommissioned in 1998.

As the College marks its Centenary five Royal Marine Bands exist and the College is extremely fortunate to have one of these based in Dartmouth. In addition to their musical duties the bandsmen are trained as medical orderlies and to assist the local community, such as the firefighting duties they were required to do in Operation Fresco during the Firefighters strikes in 2002/3.

The Voluntary College Band made up of cadets and civilians, many of them stewards, in 1955 just prior to its demise a year later when the Royal Marine Band arrived.

The Royal Marine Band concert in the Casper John Hall.

HM Royal Marine Band of Britannia Royal Naval College receives the freedom of the town of Dartmouth, 28th April 2004. The Band parades the illuminated charter, the work of Mr. Melvyn Stone, granting their freedom. Picture courtesy of South Hams Newspapers.

A posed photograph on the parade ground in full dress uniform.

The Royal Marine Band Fanfare Team.

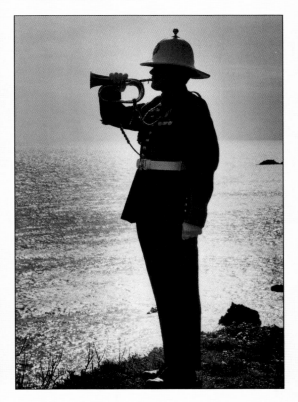

The Corps Drum Major poses for an official photograph in front of the College.

The Corps of Drums.

The Last Post.

Edward, Prince of Wales with Mr Jasper Bartlett, Chairman of the Dartmouth Harbour Commission aboard the pinnace landing at Dartmouth for the official ceremonial opening of the town's War Memorial in 1921. Reproduced by kind permission of Mrs Sally Pidsley.

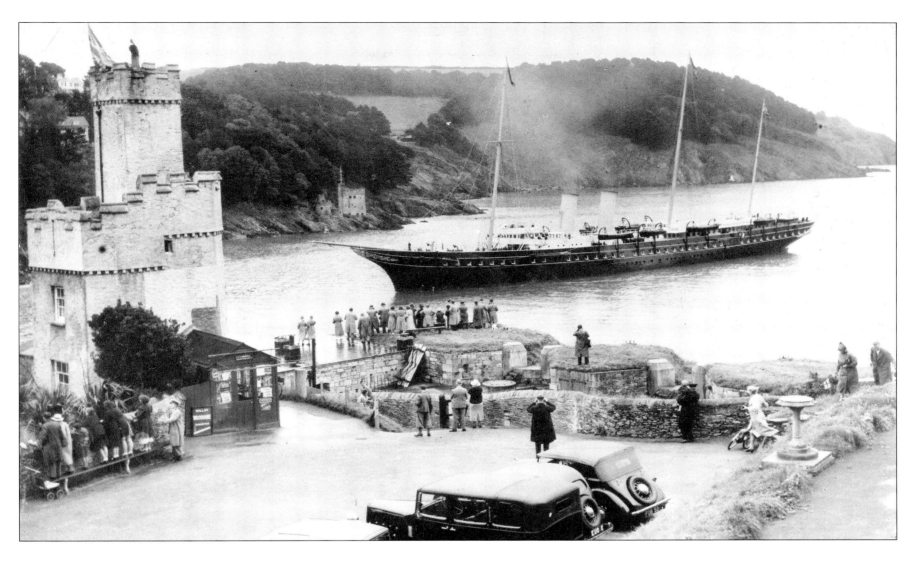

Prince Philip of Greece and the Royal Visit of 1939

The son of Prince and Princess Andrew of Greece, Prince Philip was exiled from his homeland a year after his birth, following the abdication of his uncle, King Constantine of Greece. Eventually Philip found himself in Britain, under the guardianship of Lord Milford Haven, and upon his death in 1938 Milford Haven's younger brother Lord Louis Mountbatten. During this time Philip was sent to school in Salem, Germany until the school's founder, Kurt Hahn, was forced out of the country by the Nazis. Subsequently Dr Hahn re-established his new school at Gordonstoun in Scotland, to which Philip followed. On leaving Gordonstoun, encouraged by the Mountbattens, Philip decided to join the Royal Navy. After spending some time in Cheltenham with a Mr and Mrs Mercer, to cram for the forthcoming examinations, Philip took the entrance exam to the Royal Naval College at Dartmouth, passing sixteenth out of thirty-four. Having already received a public school education Philip, aged seventeen, joined the

On Saturday 22nd July 1939 King George VI and Queen Elizabeth visited the College accompanied by their daughters the Princesses Elizabeth and Margaret. Here the Royal Yacht Victoria & Albert III *is entering the Dart and passing Dartmouth Castle. A few locals braved the wet and blustery conditions hoping to catch a sight of the Royal Family. This small group belies the fact that the visit was immensely popular with the local population as in excess of 20,000 loyal subjects turned out to greet the visitors over the two-day visit.*

'Special Entry' cadets, created by Winston Churchill in 1913 to boost numbers by recruiting young men who had already received their secondary education. These cadets were known as the 'Frobishers', after the training ship HMS *Frobisher*, on which they would normally receive their three terms' training. However, when Philip joined in May 1939, *Frobisher* was being rearmed in preparation for war so the Special Entry Cadets were housed in the Naval College to complete a foreshortened course of eight months, instead of the usual twelve.

The royal party arrives at the Town Quay in the Royal Barge. July 1939.

The royal party is introduced to the Captain of the College, and the Headmaster Mr E. W. E. Kempson, who is nearest the camera. July 1939.

Nevertheless there was still time to enjoy the pleasures of the River Dart, as the Prince fondly remembers:

'My most vivid recollection is of the boatwork in cutters and whalers. I was fortunate in having learnt to sail in a boat at my school on the Moray Firth. There was only one other cadet in my term who knew how to sail a boat. With only two term officers, we were delegated to take charge of other cadets in our term under instruction in pulling and sailing naval cutters and whalers.

I remember one occasion when four cutters were beating up the Dart on the way home, two with officers in charge and two with us in charge. At one point one of the cutters commanded by an officer made to cross my bows while he was on port tack and I was on the starboard tack. I expected him to give way, but he ploughed on, and although I did my best to go under his stern, I hit him smartly not far from where he was sitting. Fortunately no harm was done and there was no further mention of the subject!!

On another occasion I was steering a whaler in a race just outside the mouth of the river. I had discovered that the art of going-about quickly in a whaler was for the helmsman to push the yard of the mizzen to windward while holding the tiller hard down with his knees. The crew, meanwhile, were busy dipping the lug of the mainsail and shifting jib sheets. On this occasion we hit a slightly bigger wave as we went about and I was pitched overboard to leeward. Fortunately I was holding on to the mizzen sheet and managed to scramble back before anyone noticed. However they were all a bit puzzled to see me sitting in the stern sheets soaking wet.'[2]

2 Personal correspondence of HRH Prince Philip

Although brief, Philip's time at Dartmouth ended in success, culminating in the presentation of the 'King's Dirk' for best overall cadet.

However, Dartmouth was to become more than merely the gateway to a great naval career for the young prince, when in July 1939 King George VI visited the College, accompanied by Queen Elizabeth and the Princesses Elizabeth and Margaret. The true significance of the visit has become shrouded in myth, romanticism and controversy. The legend has it that this was the first time Prince Philip and Princess Elizabeth met each other and that, particularly from the latter's point of view, it was love at first sight. Certainly this is the impression given by the account of the Princesses' governess, Miss Crawford, quoting, for example, Princess Elizabeth as exclaiming 'How good he is,' as he showed off, by jumping over a tennis net. The reality however, may be more mundane.

The Royal Family had arrived at Dartmouth, in the rain, on board HMY *Victoria & Albert* on Saturday 22nd July. Among the royal party was Prince Philip's uncle, the King's *aide de camp*, Louis Mountbatten. Not unusually the College was in the middle of an epidemic of chicken-pox and mumps. It was, therefore necessary to keep the Princesses away from the risk of infection. At this point it is believed that Mountbatten intervened, suggesting that his nephew might be dragged away from his regular routine to join the Princesses. This suggestion has been interpreted as a deliberate manoeuvre on the part of Mountbatten, to throw his nephew and the future Queen together. To what extent this may be true is difficult to decipher, as a royal prince Philip was a natural choice to act as host. Mountbatten himself gave little away, noting in his diary on the first day of the visit merely that 'Philip accompanied us and dined on board' the Royal Yacht, with a number of other cadets. Next day he noted: 'Philip came back aboard *Victoria & Albert* for tea and was a great success with the children.' (Ziegler 1985, p.102.)

HM Queen Elizabeth plants a tree just to the west of the College in the grounds. The King and the two Princesses also planted trees. All of these trees still survive in what has become known as the Royal Plot. This started a tradition of royal tree planting that continues to this day.

The gallery of the gymnasium where the royal party are seen watching a demonstration by the cadets. The Princesses and the King and Queen are all seated. Behind the King, standing without a cap, is Captain Mountbatten, aide de camp to the King, and to the right of him, in a cap, is Prince Philip of Greece.

The Dartmouth visit was certainly not the first time that Philip and Elizabeth had seen each other. They had both been at George VI's coronation and at the wedding of Philip's cousin Marina in 1934. However, it is probably fair to say that at the age of thirteen this was the first time Princess Elizabeth had 'noticed' Prince Philip, even if it took some time for him fully to reciprocate the feelings of someone whom to an eighteen-year-old officer-cadet must still have appeared a child. As Mountbatten was to write many years later when advising Prince Charles on the subject of marriage: 'After all Mummy never seriously thought of anyone else after the Dartmouth encounter when she was 13.' (Ziegler 1985, p.687.)

The Captain of the College at the time, Sir Fredrick D. G. Dalrymple-Hamilton, kept a detailed diary throughout his distinguished naval career. His entries provide a fascinating insight into the visit, although they throw little light upon any emerging royal romance.

'July, 1939. Saturday 22 R.N.C.D.
V. Wet am. Showers pm.

The Royal Yacht escorted by *Keppel* (de Winton) and *Versatile* (Hussey) arrived at about 10 o'clock and secured to Nos 1 and 2 buoys. Almost as soon as she had done so the rain commenced to descend in torrents and continued doing so until about 4pm. I went aboard at 1030 and was most kindly received by the King and Queen and stayed about half an hour discussing plans and was given a glass of Port! I then returned to R.N.C. and gave orders for wet weather programme to be put into effect . . . At 3 o'clock C in C and Justina Commander and I & N Kisty and Graeme repaired to the gym. All the cadets were assembled

lining the road outside. Headmaster joined us with Revd. and Mrs Gordon (Headmaster of Blundells) and Joan (Peek). The two latter being with their respective cricket teams who had been scheduled to play here today but of course could not on account of the weather. The King and Queen and Princesses arrived at 1515 and we received them there . . . We went straight up to the gym gallery where I presented Formby and then the 9th term gave their "passing out" display and did it extremely well. Thence to the swimming bath . . . They walked down to Q.D. [quarterdeck] via D Block and officers and masters wives were presented on Q.D. after which we walked up to the Canteen stopping on the way to plant trees on the bit of grass just to the westward of west end steps. The King, Queen and Princesses each planted one and it was a rather amusing interlude. Parsloe produced shovels etc all burnished up. Then to the Canteen for tea. Headmaster next to the Queen. Others present at tea included Prince Philip of Greece, Joan, Gortons, and Seldon Cricket master at Blundells who gatecrashed and I never spotted him until after the Queen had asked who he was! Tea went off V. well with traditional Raspberries and Cream mixed with Strawberry ice – Banana and Cream and so on . . . After tea we looked at the Beagles and puppies and then made our way to Sandquay . . . All cadets were assembled there and as soon as T.M. [Their Majesties] were seated Walter Starkie started a dinghy race 21 dinghies competing . . . Then the barge came along-side and T.M. and Princesses embarked and returned to the yacht. This concluded the first day's programme at R.N.C. but in the evening T.M. gave a dinner party on the yacht . . . A wonderful party for us

all. I had the honour of sitting next to the Queen . . .
I introduced the cadets to T.M. We returned to R.N.C. about
1115 (Cadets earlier).

'July, 1939. Sunday 23
Mostly fine

The King visited escorting destroyers and arrived at our main
entrance at 1015. Cadets at Divisions. I receive H.M and H.M
the Queen and Princesses. The King walked out onto the
Bridge and was received with a Royal Salute and the Standard
was broken on the College Tower flag staff. Divisions went off
very well. Black cloud rolling up but only 1 short shower thank
God! The King presented Cups . . . Cadets marched past. The
Officers and Masters were presented on the Parade Ground.
Next off swords in the Visitors Room and Church. The
Princesses left off church owing to Mumps infection possibilities
and had a good rag in our house with North, Kisty, Graeme and
Prince Philip assisting . . . After a short interval for elevenses in
our house during which the Queen presented cakes to winning
sailing crews we went out to Parade Ground the King and
Queen went down to inspect the College employees (300 or so
mustered). They did this very thoroughly and talked to many of

*A rare private photograph of Prince Philip showing the young Princesses
the essentials of croquet on the lawn of the Captain's House. Princess
Margaret nearest to the camera and Princess Elizabeth partially hidden
behind the lady dressed in black. This was supposedly the first meeting
of Princess Elizabeth and Prince Philip.*

*The Captain, Fredrick Dalrymple-Hamilton escorts the King to the Parade
Ground for the Inspection of Divisions. The Commander of the College,
Cdr. Charles Addis is to the left behind the hand of the Captain and
Captain Mountbatten can be seen between the Captain and the King.*

them . . . Then to the Wardroom where a happy half hour and
H.M. much amused by the defaulters book etc . . . On leaving I
asked the King and Queen to look inside the Dining Hall
where cadets were all at dinner. The moment they got inside the
door the whole 500 Cadets leaped to their feet and cheered
themselves to a standstill for about 3 minutes. A quite
unrehearsed item and shook me to the core! Along the corridor
past his photograph and so to luncheon at our house . . . I sat
next to the Queen, on her left, and Prince Philip on her right.
Lady K Seymour on the King's left. Miss Crawford the
Princesses governess' on my left then Princess Margaret, Graeme,
Tommy Lascelles, Madge, H.M. the King and Lady K.S., Dickie
Mountbatten, Harold Campbell, Kisty North, Princess Elizabeth,
Prince Philip – H.M. Queen and self. After luncheon the
Princesses and young played croquet game outside. We visited
Grenville House, Seamanship Room, Library, then sick quarters,
walked through one garden then out into garden . . .
Goodbyes were said H.M. presented G and I with signed
photographs of himself and the Queen and we all walked down to
Sandquay and they re-embarked for V & A. Nothing could have
been easier than they have made this visit – We all enjoyed every
minute of it and the whole thing went with a swing despite the
weather at the beginning . . . T.M. were most kind in their
appreciation of all they had seen. The event of the evening was the
send off to the Yacht. Cadets [including Prince Philip] manned
every boat we had in the place and the whole party proceeded to
lie off the starboard side of the Yacht . . . Whilst we were waiting a
blue dinghy was called alongside and a message lowered into it. This
contained a signal from H.M. the King giving 4 extra days leave at

The March – Past after the Inspection of Divisions and the King is taking the Salute. This area is known as the Bridge, and on it can be seen the headmaster, Mr Kempson, his staff in their gowns and mortarboards are to the left of the Bridge, with the officers to the right. The practice of wearing academic dress at Divisions is still continued to this day. In the distance in the garden of the Captain's House can be seen one of the Princesses.

The King inspecting Divisions on a very wet and blustery 23rd July 1939. The Royal Yacht can be seen anchored in the Bight in the distance.

the end of the summer holidays and a request to me to impart the news there and then which I did to all the boats round and produced a splendid storm of cheering. Later on when V & A was aweigh we gave more cheers for King and Queen . . . We then slipped all boats as V & A gathered way they all rowed their hardest and the whole party accompanied her to sea . . . We followed until she stopped to drop the pilot and then as she got under way again one final cheer and turned towards her and so back. It was a wonderful sight and I shall never forget it seeing the old yacht steaming along slowly with all the boats accompanying her and the King and Queen and Princesses on the bridge waving and everyone cheering and so ended our much looked forward to Royal Visit and we returned to our harbour and college tired and pleased with ourselves and everybody else but particularly so with our Visitors who couldn't have made a greater success of the whole visit.'

Thus the summer term of 1939 came successfully to a conclusion. However, by the time the College returned for the autumn term Britain was once again at war. The Second World War would see even greater losses for the Royal Navy than the first. Amongst those involved were former royal cadets Lord Mountbatten, the Duke of Kent, Prince Philip and of course HM King George VI, who won the respect and admiration of his people as he led them through the nation's darkest hours until victory in 1945. After the war the tradition of royal princes at Dartmouth was to continue when Prince Charles joined Dartmouth on 16th September 1971, as a member of Blake Division. Prince Andrew followed his elder brother to Dartmouth as a member of Hawke Division in September 1979. A hundred and two years since Princes Edward and George had first stepped on board *Britannia* in 1877 the Naval College could once again claim to be truly Royal.

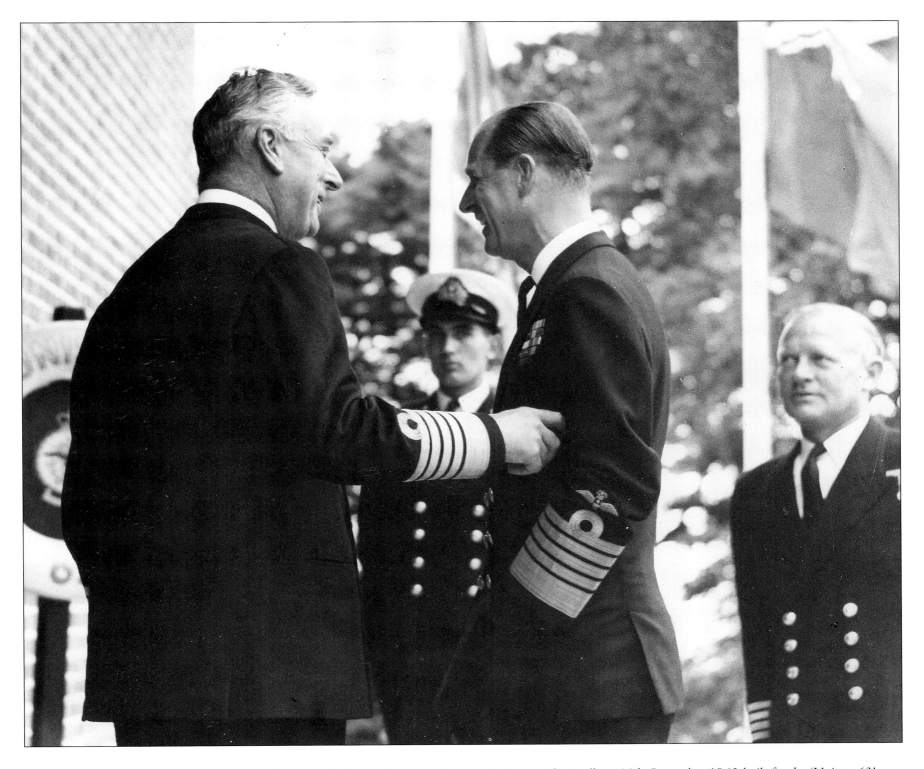

Lord Louis Mountbatten shares a moment with Prince Philip outside the newly opened Casper John Hall on 11th September 1963 built for the 'Unison 63' gathering of senior representatives of the Commonwealth Armed Forces.

Following pages: 'Memories' - watercolour by Michael Hill based upon the reminiscences of former cadets of the College. Published as a limited edition print by Barbican Gallery, Plymouth.

His Royal Highness the Prince of Wales

Above: Prince Charles at a Passing Out Parade in 1971.

Right: HRH Prince Charles arrives at the College to commence his training. The term had started the previous day but Charles arrived in his Aston Martin and drew up on the Bridge to be greeted by the Captain of the College, Captain Allan Tait. 16th September 1971.

Above: Prince Charles aboard one of the College yachts near Dartmouth Castle.

*P*rince Charles joined Dartmouth on 16th September 1971, as a member of Blake Division, having completed a period of service with the RAF. As a graduate entrant, he spent just six weeks at the College, learning about leadership, navigation and the ways of the Royal Navy. In common with many graduate students at the time Prince Charles found the constraints of Dartmouth irksome: 'It was exactly like being locked up at school again and we weren't allowed out, except on rare weekends. It really was quite a business . . . endless rushing about, drill . . . quite a shock to the system.' (Dimbleby, 1994, p. 196.) He was, though, popular among his classmates who identified with his self-deprecating manner and his willingness to join in. At the time, he may have been relieved that he was only to suffer the pressures of Dartmouth for a short spell, but he later agreed with changes to the training pattern, which resulted in extended courses for all young officers, admitting that as a Naval Officer he would have benefited from a longer stay: 'There is no substitute for professional training'. (Winton, 1981 p. 90). Although he did not consider himself to be a natural seaman, Prince Charles was a proficient handler of the College picket boats on the river, experience that was to underpin his effectiveness and professional flair in command of the minehunter HMS Bronington in 1976, his final appointment in the Senior Service.

His Royal Highness the Duke of York

The Duke of York followed his elder brother to Dartmouth for two terms in September 1979, joining as a short service Seaman Officer, specialising as a pilot. He was in Hawke Division, which at the time was housed in the old sick quarters. Like his elder brother before him, Prince Andrew applied himself to his studies and performed well, even finding time and energy to complete successfully commando training at the Royal Marine Commando Training Centre, Lympstone. Prince Andrew proudly received the coveted Green Beret one week before passing out from Dartmouth, in front of Her Majesty The Queen, at Lord High Admiral's Divisions. Unlike his elder brother with prior responsibilities as heir to the throne, Prince Andrew was in a position to make the Navy a longer career. In 1982, as a member of 820 Naval Air squadron he embarked in the aircraft carrier HMS Invincible, he followed in his father's and grandfather's footsteps, going to war in the South Atlantic to retake the Falkland Islands. Subsequently, he served in various appointments, including frigates and commanding a mine countermeasures vessel, before earning promotion to Commander and seeing service in the Ministry of Defence. Prince Andrew finally stepped outside the Service to other State duties in 2002.

HRH The Prince Andrew at the front door to the College while he was under training from September 1979 to April 1980.

Above: Passing Out Platoon marching with Prince Andrew on the back row nearest the camera. April 1980.

Right: On the ceiling of the Wardroom at the College, there are three signatures, Prince Charles, Prince Andrew and Prince Edward (at BRNC for a short introductory course while with the Royal Marines). 'Signing the ceiling', or deckhead as it is known at College is one of the after mess-dinner pastimes of Naval Officers. Indeed legend has it that the deckhead was covered with signatures before it was painted over and just three left. The method of signing is to support the signatory with the aid of a human pyramid. In this rare private photograph, Prince Andrew can be seen 'in action'. More than one officer has suffered broken bones in the past from this and other precarious stunts.

(All Sub-Lieutenants : from left to right)

Sixth row :   G R Philpot, B P S Brooks, J M Burnell-Nugent, K S Brimley
Fifth row :   S T Howes, W R Stewart, P R Davies, P R Budd, C J Hill, A S Kern, P Addison
Fourth row :   P B Towl, H G Wylie, N S Pattenden, H J R Milner, A W T Sanders, R A M Richards, M A Giddings
Third row :   R J Etty, G R Buck, P V Hunt, G E Gill, C M L C Hayward, C W Hattersley, K M Heynes, P R Engeham
Second row :   R T Springthorpe, G D A Richardson, D E Ledger, A C Slater, M A Barge, I B Deane, T J Hines, M J Kay, R S Saxby
Front row :   J B Binns, P R Freeman, J C Davidson, The Prince of Wales, Lt-Cdr R T Frere, Lt-Cdr J Bird, C M Wrigley, G Alsop, F H Hiscock, R G Lockwood

Term photograph with Prince Charles in the front row, the fourth from the left.

CHAPTER 5

The College at War

As the inscription on the front of the College reminds us, the Royal Navy has for centuries provided the wealth, prosperity and peace, upon which Britain has depended to build an empire and spread international trade. In the course of providing the basis for Britain's international power the Navy has inevitably found itself required to go beyond the protection of sea-lanes of communication and play a critical, often decisive, role in the defence of the homeland. Though it may be a less than comfortable thought for those employed at the Royal Navy's College, whether staff officer, academic or student, the ultimate function of the Navy is to go to war in support of the nation's interests. The ultimate function of the Royal Naval College is therefore to educate Naval Officers for the prospect of finding themselves on the front line.

The first half of the College's history was to be punctuated by two world wars, each of which would have a very profound but very different impact upon the College and its population. In many respects it is no coincidence that the First World War broke out as the College began its tenth academic year. The founding of the shore-based College and Admiral Fisher's revolutionary new system of naval education that accompanied it were intricately linked to Britain's perceived need to counter the German Kaiser's growing naval ambitions.

The telegram received by the Captain of the College at 3.50pm on 1st August 1914, from the Commander in Chief Portsmouth, ordering the College to 'mobilise.'

The First World War

On Monday 27th July 1914, the College received a telegram ordering it to standby to mobilise. The next day Austria, having failed to secure the demands of its ultimatum from the Serbian government as recompense for the assassination of their heir to the throne and assured of German support, declared war on Serbia. But as relations among the great powers continued to deteriorate and the armies of Europe began to mobilise, life at Dartmouth carried on as usual. The end of term was approaching and final examinations were underway. By the end of the week hope was fading of the prospect that war might interrupt the College routine. Then at 3.50pm on Saturday 1st August, as a cricket match was being played on the playing field, Captain Victor Stanley received a telegram which simply read; 'mobilise.'

Cadets' sea chests at the back of B block packed and ready for transportation having received the order to 'mobilise' on Saturday 1st August 1914.

The earlier telegram meant that cadets' sea chests had already been packed and orders placed with local vehicle owners to transport the cadets and their belongings down to the railway pontoon. From there they would take the Great Western Railway's ferry boat, the *Mew*, to the railway station in Kingswear, where three trains were standing by to take cadets off to join their appointed ships in Plymouth, Portsmouth and Chatham. Cadets, officers and masters all helped with the loading of chests onto the various assembled vehicles. Soon the line of vehicles loaded with luggage covered almost the entire length of the northern embankment. Cadets marched to the *Mew* in their respective terms, cheered on by large crowds of residents. The first to leave were those with the longest journey ahead of them, the Third and Fourth Terms bound for Chatham. The Portsmouth train went next, carrying the Second and Fifth Terms. Finally the Plymouth train departed Kingswear at 10.46pm, taking the First and Sixth Terms together with nearly two hundred reservists from the ship's company. That night only the officers and masters remained at the College.

However, the speed and efficiency with which the College had mobilised seems not to have been repeated further along the line. The Portsmouth bound cadets had to be turned back, their ships unready

to take them. Their return to Dartmouth was, however brief. Having arrived back at seven o'clock on the Sunday morning they were excused church and that evening departed once again for Portsmouth. Meanwhile at Devonport cadets found themselves sleeping on the floor of the wardroom. The following day turned out wet, with nothing to do but wander around the dockyard admiring the ships, even the church service was cut short as a result of the impending war. But war could not interrupt the completion of naval education, on 3rd August Sixth Term cadets sat their final passing out exam at the Royal Naval Engineering College, Keyham. The next day neutral Belgium was invaded and Britain declared war on Germany.

Captain Stanley's response to the outbreak of war was swift, the College's miniature rifle range was to be open to the public from 10am to 1pm and 2pm to 6pm daily, while for those requiring a little extra tuition the following notice appearing in the town:

'England is at War. Every man should be able to defend his home and use a rifle. The Officers remaining at the College will gladly take drill classes at 3.30 and 6.30 today [5th August]. Volunteers should assemble in front of the College at either of these hours.'

The response was tremendous, the assembled crowd including

The GWR ferry the Mew*, which took Cadets from Dartmouth to Kingswear where they met the trains which would take them to join their appointed ships. This photograph is believed to show troops from the 7th Battalion London Regiment later in 1914.*

the Deputy Mayor, Alderman R. Row, and several other members of the town council, professional men, tradesmen, shop assistants, mechanics and others, all eager to defend their homeland. Captain Stanley addressed them:

'I am very glad indeed to see such a response to the appeal sent out this morning. I am not going to detain you long because I am of the opinion, and I expect it is the opinion of everyone here, that it is a time for deeds not words.' (Applause.) 'It is very easy to attain a certain amount of proficiency with a rifle ... a very short time will suffice. There are a few officers of the College left – only two or three – and there are two or three masters and they are willing to show you how to handle a rifle, for the time may come for you to make use of one.' (*Britannia Magazine*, July 1964.)

By this time there were in fact few officers or masters left at the College. Of the naval staff only the Fleet Surgeon and one naval instructor remained, Captain Stanley himself was soon re-deployed to take command of the ex-Turkish battleship HMS *Erin*, to be temporarily replaced at Dartmouth by Rear Admiral Napier. The College itself, it seemed, might be made ready to act as a hospital for the Grand Fleet, to take care of the casualties of the impending great naval engagement that was expected. However, at the beginning of September it was announced that seventy-five Osborne cadets, and three Conway cadets, would be arriving on the seventeenth (*Dartmouth Chronicle*, 4/9/1914). Only the Headmaster, two heads of department and four other masters would be left to teach them and fill in the gaps left by the staff officers called up into the fleet. At both Dartmouth and Osborne masters took over the duties of term officers, wearing a sort of uniform/academic dress hybrid, consisting of blue suit and mortarboards on divisions (or when officers wore white cap-covers, straw boaters); a system which seems to have worked well. Of the rest

Memorial tablet to Midshipman H. L. Riley, lost in HMS Aboukir *September 22nd 1914, aged 15 years.*

of the academic staff, nine joined the services, including M. Charbonnier of Modern Languages who joined the French army, and eleven were sent to Osborne, which became the focus of naval education. Two more were co-opted to join a new organisation. Sir Alfred Ewing, a Professor of Mechanical Engineering at Cambridge University before being appointed as Director of Naval Education by Fisher, had been approached by Admiral Oliver, Director of Naval Intelligence, to set up an organisation to interpret German signals intelligence. To man this organisation, which became known as Room 40, Ewing turned to his colleagues in the Mathematics and Modern Languages departments at Osborne and Dartmouth. William H. Anstie and Denis Bond were the first recruits, followed in 1915 by A. G. Denniston from Osborne, who went on to become head of Bletchley Park during the Second World War, E. C. J. Green in 1916 and in 1918 by R. P. Keigwin. All these individuals' names were

Passing out photographs from RNC Osborne (these cadets were never to actually pass-out from Dartmouth so these are the only photographs), including twelve of those who died on HMS Aboukir, Cressy *and* Hogue *in September 1914.*

retained on the College Blue Lists, referred to as 'serving at Admiralty.'

At the outbreak of war 434 Dartmouth cadets had been sent, enthusiastically, to sea. They were not however, destined for the pride of the Grand Fleet but as not yet fully-trained naval officers were to find themselves on board older, less capable, more vulnerable vessels. Thus the realities of war were very quickly brought home. On 22nd September the three British cruisers, HMS *Aboukir*, *Hogue* and *Cressy*, were torpedoed in the North Sea by a German submarine, *U-9*. Among the 1,459 officers and men killed were thirteen cadets or midshipmen who seven weeks earlier had left Dartmouth. They were aged between fifteen and sixteen and a half years old. The *Osborne Magazine* records those who had been lost:[1]

1 Throughout the war the *Osborne Magazine* pays more attention to the war than its *Britannia* counterpart. This is perhaps natural as many of the boys sent to sea, who had completed their education at Osborne did not complete their time at Dartmouth.

2 J. A. Froude was the grandson of the historian James Froude of Salcombe and the great nephew of the engineer William Froude (1810-1879). William Froude joined the practice of I. K. Brunel in 1837. In 1844 he worked on the South Devon atmospheric railway, but moved to Dartington Parsonage in 1846 to look after his ailing father. Thereafter Brunel employed him on special projects such as the motion of ships and screw propellers. He went on the maiden voyage of the *Great Eastern* and did work on her stability.

H.M.S. *Aboukir*
Cadet J. D. Stubbs
Cadet G. Gore-Brown
Cadet G. B. Barchard
Cadet A. V. G. Allsopp
Cadet H. L. Riley

H.M.S. *Cressy*
Midshipman C. P. Dalmege
Midshipman V. H. Corbyn
Midshipman F. G. Matthews
Midshipman J. A. Froude[2]

H.M.S. *Hogue*
Midshipman H. H. Ward
Midshipman G. C. Harold
Midshipman C. W. Holt

Amongst the controversy as to how these ageing vessels had been allowed to patrol unprotected and unprepared for engagement with the enemy, questions were also raised as to the rationale behind sending boys to sea. The case was taken up by Mr W. Joynson-Hicks, Conservative MP for Brentford, who wrote a letter to the *Morning Post* criticising the First Lord of the Admiralty, Winston Churchill:

'It must be understood that I am not speaking of Midshipmen who are not gazetted younger than 17 but of children who can do no possible good on board men-of-war in time of action . . . Their room would be much more valuable on board than their presence [for example, stories told of German prisoners having to sleep, and die, lying under cadets' hammocks after the battle of Heligoland Bight].

Perhaps the Admiralty answer would be that it is desirable to harden boys but if Mr Churchill will only apply to the officers in command of cruisers where these boys are, I think he will be told that they would be better sent back to complete their education at Dartmouth, and that by so doing they will preserve the supply of officers for the navy of the future which is seriously endangered by the result of the disasters such as we are bound to expect in the course of a prolonged and difficult war.' (*Dartmouth Chronicle*, 2/10/1914.)

Other accounts, however, suggest a more positive contribution to the war effort. Cadets Riley and Stubbs of *Aboukir* had died while going to the assistance of a drowning man who had taken them under, while the newly-commissioned Midshipman Cazalet of the *Cressy*, using a whaler, had picked up eighty-eight survivors from the *Cressy* and *Hogue*, including the *Cressy*'s commander. The official Admiralty response was also unrepentant about the decision, made sometime before the outbreak of war, to discharge cadets from Dartmouth to help relieve the reserve fleet. As Churchill explained to the House of Commons, it was felt that these young officers would be very useful on board ship as part of the regular complement, and that they would learn far more of their profession at sea than they would at any educational establishment. As for their return to Dartmouth, that would depend largely on the duration of the war and was felt to be unlikely. Meanwhile, any future decisions to send cadets from Dartmouth to sea would depend upon the operational requirements of the fleet. Nevertheless, by the beginning of 1915 of those 434 cadets who had marched singing and cheering to meet their trains at Kingswear, forty-one had lost their lives, a greater proportion than any other class of naval officer in the fleet (*Dartmouth Chronicle*, 12/2/1915.)

Ironically, while at sea cadets and midshipmen were officially considered as undergoing continued naval training. Consequently their parents were still expected to pay a fifty pounds allowance to the Admiralty. When questioned in the House, Dr Macnamara replied on behalf of the Admiralty that;

'it would be prepared to give favourable consideration to applications for whole or partial relief where necessity exists, and further, that in the case of midshipmen killed in active service any sums deposited in advance in a period subsequent to the death are returned to the guardians upon the closing of the private allowance accounts of the officers concerned.' (*Dartmouth Chronicle* 26/2/1915.)

Those in this photograph had only just completed their first term at Dartmouth and many of them were barely fifteen years old. By the time the war was over most of the cadets from 1914 would have seen service in the Grand Fleet, being involved in the Gallipoli landings and the Battle of Jutland.

Midshipmen's Journals

*O*n completion of their time at Dartmouth the newly commissioned midshipmen remained under training on board their first ship. During this time they were required to keep a journal, or diary, of the day-to-day life of the most junior officer in the Royal Navy. The College archive retains a selection of these journals, dating from the mid-nineteenth to mid-twentieth centuries. Of particular historical interest is the collection of Second World War journals, many of which chronicle some of the major events of the war at sea, from the Battle of the River Plate to the D-Day landings. During the War it was necessary to impound journals completed by midshipmen during their training on board cruisers and destroyers of the fleet. Such journals would contain classified materials and information about Allied operations. The Naval College was one of the holding authorities of these impounded journals, some of which were not collected at the end of the War and therefore remained in the College archive. History aside these journals also demonstrate the dedication and in may cases real artistic and literary talents of their authors.

Midshipman P H Owen HMS Royal Oak, Scapa Flow, 14th October 1939

Mid. Owen had joined Royal Oak *on 25th August 1939, straight from Dartmouth. On the night of the 13th-14th October the ship was lying at berth in Scapa Flow, when she came under attack from a German U-boat. Owen's journal recalls the night's events:*

'It was about 0120…that the first tremendous explosion woke up the Ship's Company. The general assumption was that a bomb hit us and many men manned the A.A. stations; others went under armour; but very many turned over and went back to sleep again…

'The Midshipmen had just been shaken by the instructor Lieutenant when at 0140 three or possibly four shattering explosions occurred at about 3 second intervals and the ship immediately started listing to starboard…

'Twenty minutes after the ship had first been torpedoed no definite steps had been taken by anyone to save the ship or her company, and there was no more time as the final explosion had caused her to keel over very rapidly – she was uppermost 7 minutes later, according to witnesses in the *Pegasus*.

'As the ship started listing the lights went out, and the ladders grew progressively more difficult for everyman to negotiate – and virtually impossible for the 1100 odd men trapped below…

'The picket boat got away and picked up about 60 men and all went well until the officer in charge told these men to paddle, causing the boat to roll on her beam ends, shaking off several people, who finally capsized the outfit by trying to climb back…The only man to reach the launch at her boom was the Midshipman of the boat, who unfortunately was not able to clear her before she was pulled under as she was moored up by too short a strop…

— H.M.S. JACKAL —

A POM-POM'S CREW IN ACTION.

'In the water there must have been about 600 men, of whom very many were picked up by the drifter off the port quarter and beam. Others met their fate with the picket boat and quite a number were picked up by the boats from the *Pegasus*. 15 men reached the shore and the remaining were drowned. The Flow was extremely cold and there was very little wreckage about; on the starboard side the oil fuel was very oppressive indeed and many men brought up solid fuel for hours afterwards.'

Midshipman G R Shaw HMS Rodney, May 1941

Mid. G R Shaw had joined Dartmouth in May 1939, two years later he found himself on board HMS Rodney *as she joined the chase to sink the* Bismarck.

'Tuesday 27th May – The Commander-in-Chief signalled he was going to work round to the westward and attack at dawn, while torpedo attacks by the destroyers were carried out under cover of darkness…

'The long wait throughout the night was somewhat trying, but soon after dawn I climbed the 6th D.C.T. and settled down. At 0800 the destroyers of the 4th Flotilla came in sight and at 0845 *Norfolk* could be seen on the horizon. It would only be a few minutes until we sighted *Bismarck*.

'The ADP reported her to be on the starboard bow, the aloft director was soon bearing, and a minute later the 16-inch opened fire. *King George V* on our starboard beam followed immediately with her main armament.

'A few seconds later the Captain altered course to starboard and I got my first view of the enemy through my glasses. She was steering towards us with an inclination of about 160 right and looked a huge ship. We saw our 16-inch fall round her, then two flashes as she opened fire at *Rodney*, at the same time altering course to starboard. We opened fire with the 6-inch at 20,000 yards

and by this time it had ceased fire and her control top was burning momentarily. She looked very impressive – huge splashes coming up all round her, while she came on towards us the seas sweeping off the huge flare on her bows…'

'When we altered course for what turned out to be the last run on the port side, *Bismarck* was a grand but ghastly sight. Water poured from the numerous holes in her bows as she rose clear of the seas. Her guns were lying drunkenly at all angles, upperworks smashed and blowing, smoke pouring from the funnel, flames licking round her barbettes and numerous flashes denoting our shells were hitting, while 'shorts' and 'overs' threw up a cascade of water all around the doomed vessel…

'The enemy turned and sank when we were about three miles away and *Hood's* loss was avenged. Considering the odds against her and the disabilities she was already suffering from, *Bismarck* put up a great fight, and her builders were undoubtedly justified when they claimed her to be the most powerful warship afloat. She was the finest looking ship I have ever seen, and it was pitiful to see her in the final phase of the action beaten and battered but still giving the impression of immense power.'

— H.M.S. REVENGE —

All these illustrations are taken from the journal of Midshipman D. V. M. Moore. Clearly a gifted artist, Moore found himself in the North Atlantic and English Channel on board HMS *Revenge* between May 1940 and October 1941.

Meanwhile, back at Dartmouth, two Terms joined from Osborne in January 1915, bringing the College population up to 236. From April that year there were four Terms, rising to five in September 1916, when 121 cadets who had joined Osborne in 1914 moved up to the senior College. Despite this huge increase in numbers, reaching a peak of 535 in May 1918, cadets would only actually spend three terms (one year) in the College, rather than the pre-war six (two years), before being sent to sea.

In order to accommodate the projected rise in the number of cadets, work began as early as 1914 to build an extra accommodation block, to become known as D block. However, as the war effort continued labour around Dartmouth became increasingly scarce. In order to attract labourers it was therefore necessary to offer higher wages, a strategy that was met with hostility by local farmers who were unable to compete. D block was finally opened in 1917, just in time to accommodate the great increase in the number of students.

In June 1916 Dartmouth was to suffer yet another casualty of war. Since the shore based College opened HMS *Britannia* had continued to lie in the River Dart. In February 1915 she had been sold to Messers Hughes, Bolckow & Co. of Blyth. Work had begun to remove the top hamper and upper works; the figurehead was also removed to eventually find its resting-place ashore. A public outcry ensued, leading to the setting up of a 'Britannia Fund,' which secured the option to buy the old hulk for the nation and possibly turn it into an orphanage for servicemen's children. However, such were the demands of the war effort that finally it was decided that the old ship should be broken up so as to provide copper, iron and lead for conversion into munitions.

Throughout the war, for those who remained at the College, life had continued as normally as possible, save the occasional alert caused by the sighting of a German trawler[3]. Finally, on 11th November 1918 the College received news of the cessation of hostilities. The editor of the *Britannia Magazine* summed up the sentiments of the time:

' "The war is won," and the world will not forget the part the British Navy played. Nor shall we in our rejoicings forget those naval officers of every rank from Admiral to Cadet who have given their lives for the great Ideal.' (*Britannia Magazine*, December 1918).

The academic and naval staff of the College outside the canteen (now the pavilion) in the autumn of 1941. Notably many of the civilians are wearing uniform, principally that of the Home Guard. The Captain R L B Cunliffe is in the centre of the second row, with the Headmaster, E W E Kempson on his right. The second Director of Studies, G W E Ghey is also pictured, second from the right on the second row, as is the first woman on the staff, Second Officer Morris, the Captain's secretary, who is in front of the Captain.

3 See The Royal College Chapter 4.

The Second World War

Tragically the optimism that followed the end of the Great War was to be short lived. Just two decades later another generation of aspiring naval officers was to find itself, along with the rest of the world, dragged into a second, deadlier conflict. Once again, the Royal Navy would be called upon to fight, not just for the British Empire but for the preservation of civilisation.

The summer term of 1939 at Dartmouth had passed tranquilly enough, culminating in the royal visit of the King and Queen and their two daughters to the College. The visit was regarded as a great success and when the royal party left in the royal yacht *Victoria and Albert*, it was accompanied by cadets manning every boat the college could muster. The royal party was cheered heartily as they sailed out of the harbour. A dinghy was called alongside the yacht and a message lowered to it. It contained a signal from the King giving an extra four days leave at the end of the summer holidays, thus inspiring further cheers from the cadets. However, by the time they returned to the College in September Britain was at war.

The disruption and major changes that had marked the start of the First World War at the College were not repeated in 1939. College life continued much as it had done in peacetime and the changes were initially much more gradual. The German navy was unready for war in 1939 and did not have a large capital fleet ready for action. Consequently the regular Dartmouth cadets were not required to mobilise as the Royal Naval Reserve (RNR) and Royal Naval Volunteer Reserve (RNVR) could be relied upon along with the Special Entry cadets.

Unlike 1914 the College retained many of its officers, although the principle had been established that they would be drawn mainly from the retired list and from those medically unfit from the active list. The result was not unwelcome to cadets, who found the older 're-treads' more kindly disposed than the younger, keener house officers, being no longer concerned by the prospect of promotion (Holloway 1993, p.26). Captain Dalrymple-Hamilton was replaced after approximately two months of the first term of the war and the Commander a month later, thus ensuring some continuity of the senior officers and avoiding the situation that was inflicted upon the College in 1914 when the College was stripped of senior officers. The new Captain of the College was R.B.L. Cunliffe, the first Captain to have been a cadet at the shore based College, all previous commanding officers having been from the *Britannia*. The Commander and the First Lieutenant were both replaced by officers from the retired list, as were several other appointments. These were the first real changes, but one of the most obvious transformations was amongst the masters, many of whom began to wear the uniform of the Home Guard while others left to join the regular armed forces. Other noticeable changes included the blacked out windows, which at least meant curtains for the previously bare windows, and

A Wren receives instruction on a two pound 'pom-pom' gun, thought to be on the top of D block.

Cadets filling sandbags outside D block, in anticipation of an attack.

as further air raid precautions the painted figurehead of *Britannia* on the parade ground, originally white, was painted black while the concrete parade ground itself was covered in asphalt. Those masters in the Home Guard formed their own unit in Dartmouth, and as befitted their position, were all made officers, one Captain and all the others Lieutenants. Their duties usually included guarding key sites such as the water tower on the hill above the town.

Meanwhile among the cadets, difficulties with the laundry led to shorts replacing white flannel trousers as part of the daily rig. Rationing also began to hit provisions in the Gunroom. A notice read that 'from Friday onwards milk will be rationed. It will be mixed with the tea and coffee. At breakfast 10 jugs of milk will be allocated to each table for use with porridge only. Milk is not available as a separate drink.' Worse was to come, as one line book entry commented despondently: 'lamb stew (staple food of the Cadets at the Royal Naval College) is now made out of leaves, as is borne out by the above (sic) specimen found in the portion of lamb 'stoo' assigned to Cadet Gettez'.

In February 1940 the recently re-appointed First Lord of the Admiralty, Sir Winston Churchill, visited the College while in the area to welcome home the damaged HMS *Exeter* after her success at the Battle of the River Plate. In a morale-boosting visit, he inspected the cadets and afterwards addressed them from the upper gallery of the Quarterdeck. During the visit the First Lord enquired of the history master, Mr Ted Hughes, how much history was taught. He was clearly pleased with the answer, replying 'I am very glad to hear that you teach so much history: it is the one guide to the future' he then paused and added, almost to himself, 'that and imagination'.

By the spring of 1940 the war was really starting to disrupt the College routine. The location of the College, the shipyard at Noss and the fact that Dartmouth and Kingswear were used as bunkering ports for the coaling of ships, made Dartmouth a prime target for air raids. Precautions had to be taken. The clock bells were silenced and barbed wire was placed around the buildings. Senior cadets were arranged into watches to cover fire parties and demolition and decontamination squads. These duties also continued through leave, with cadets divided in two, half of whom stayed on two weeks after the end of term and the others being recalled two weeks before the start of the next term. Routine was very much relaxed during these periods, although uniform was still worn. The summer leave, with its longer days of daylight was excluded from this procedure, which was eventually abandoned altogether. House officers were issued with ammunition and hand grenades to be kept in their rooms should there be an attack at night. A Special Service Company of local volunteers was formed, comprising sixty men who were trained in the use of revolvers and rifles, sten gun handling and grenade throwing. Cadets were also employed to make sandbags, which were deployed around the College, just as they had been in the autumn of 1938 in response to the Munich crisis. On that occasion the

preparation of College defences had been the cause of much excitement, as the Blake Line Book of the time describes:

'Parties were detailed off to do various jobs. Two groups of large cadets were marched off like 'iron guards' carrying picks and shovels at the slope. One lot went and filled sandbags; the others worked on the bank outside. A third party of smaller people carried and piled the bags into protective ramparts for A.R.P. stations. Intensive energy and excitement prevailed in all quarters, since we never knew whether we might be mobilised and rushed off the next day, or the College bombed within the next week.'

The buildings were also beginning to show signs that Britain was at war. The service passages beneath the building were utilised as air raid shelters, but they were cramped and carried the heating pipes and as such were not ideal for the new use, hence a number of shelters were built in the grounds. Some of these still exist and are used as storage areas. The upper dormitories were vacated and the ground floor boot rooms were cleared so that they could be used as sleeping areas.

At the outbreak of war the Admiralty had appointed a retired naval officer to the position of 'Naval Officer in Charge' (NOIC) of the port of Dartmouth, his jurisdiction extending along the coast from Salcombe in South Devon to Beer in East Devon. In early 1940 this position of NOIC Dartmouth was combined with that of Captain of the College. It was not long before the spaces vacated in the College began to be filled with the expanding NOIC's staff and a large contingent from the WRNS. The Wrens manned a telephone exchange, operations room and wireless transmitting station in the space under the terrace facing the parade ground. Huts were erected around the grounds for gunnery and torpedo training, the band practice room was commandeered as an aircraft recognition centre and even the beagles gave up their kennels so that pigs could be kept to help with the war effort.

Inevitably, the fortunes of the Royal Navy throughout the war had their impact on the cadets. On 14th October 1939, HMS *Royal Oak* was sunk by a German U-boat in Scapa Flow. Amongst the 809 men and twenty-four officers who lost their lives were midshipmen who had only left Dartmouth the previous summer; 'that did more than anything else to bring home to us what war was all about – killing and being killed' (Holloway 1993, p.27). An entry in the Exmouth Line Book of 1941 recalls that 'Philip Peck, cadet captain of the Exmouth House, and chief cheerer for the 'mumps' ward when the King and Queen visited [in 1939] has drowned while serving as a Midshipman in HMS *Wryneck*[4]. We are all saddened'.

In May 1940 the war really came to Dartmouth. One former cadet recalls walking onto the Quarterdeck and being struck by an unfamiliar smell. It was the odour of the 'unwashed human bodies, particularly feet' (Holloway 1993, p.33) belonging to soldiers of the British Expeditionary Force, recently evacuated from Dunkirk.

4 The destroyer HMS *Wryneck* was sunk off Greece in 1941

These photographs were all taken by Mr John Barlee MSc. a master and lecturer at the College from 1939 to 1976. Although at the time of the first bombing the College had not resumed from its summer break, Mr Barlee was working in one of the classrooms off the Quarterdeck, formerly known as the Great Hall, on the morning of 18th September 1942. He was almost half way between where the two bombs fell. After the second bomb he managed to vacate the classroom, where remarkably, only the soles of his shoes were damaged. He found a group digging frantically for someone buried in the rubble, "we are looking for Mr Barlee" they said as they had not recognised the figure of Mr Barlee, completely covered in dust, standing next to them. Being a keen photographer Mr Barlee collected his camera from the Common Room and took these photographs.

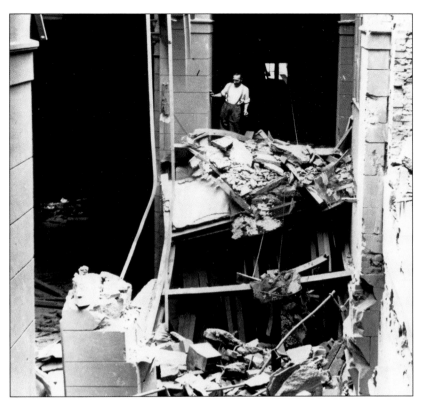

Right: The western side of the gallery destroyed, feet from where the second bomb fell.

Debris from the collapsed roof of the Quarterdeck, looking towards the corner classroom where John Barlee was when the two bombs fell.

During the following summer leave two companies of the Durham Light Infantry were housed in the College to be refitted and rehabilitated after their experiences. Meanwhile the River Dart was crammed with fishing trawlers from France, Belgium and Holland. Among them were two French tugs, which were taken over and commissioned with their own crews to work on the river. While these French ships were in Dartmouth a daily news sheet was organised, typed and distributed to them by cadets. In July 1940 it was decided that all French naval ships had to be taken over and their crews given the option of joining the Free French or being returned to France. Cadets provided the armed guards and the ships' companies were taken to the Guildhall where a statement was read to them giving them this option. According to Captain Cunliffe, writing in the *Britannia Magazine* in 1947: 'Not many volunteered to join the Free French but the incident passed off without any trouble but it was a terrible thing to have to do.' (*Britannia Magazine*, Easter 1947, p.6)

The French were not the only visitors to Dartmouth. In October 1941 twenty Norwegian Cadets were attached to the Special Entry. They were subsequently visited by HM The King of Norway and the Crown Prince, who spent a weekend at the College. Sixty years later HRH Crown Prince Haakon was to take the salute at Lord High Admiral's Divisions.

With the fall of France, the invasion of England appeared imminent. Beach defences, gun emplacements, search-lights, harbour booms and torpedo defences were constructed all along the south coast. In South Devon these were the responsibility of NOIC Dartmouth and consequently involved the College. The mobile naval battery was located at the College for a time and when the Dartmouth battery was ready, before the gun crew could arrive, a group of senior cadets took charge for a few days and fired several trial rounds, an exciting prospect for the cadets involved. Other cadets found themselves being deployed on the streets of Dartmouth to guard against fifth columnists, although quite what they were to do should they meet any was never elaborated upon! The College was also used for exercises, usually for the Commandos quartered in the neighbourhood to capture the College and port, as reported in the Exmouth Line Book:

'A mock battle took place, in which 800 soldiers took part with the College as the objective. Some of the attackers crossed the river in boats, others came from the direction of Norton, all were armed with Tommy guns, rifles, dummy grenades etc with blank ammunition. Various umpires gauged the progress of the fighting and with great difficulty allotted casualties. At the end of the afternoon it was decided that the hospital had been captured, but elsewhere the attackers had been repulsed with heavy losses'.

As Captain Cunliffe recalled, however, there was not always fair play: 'On one occasion the enemy was deemed to have cheated, as they drove through our patrols in a hearse, the coffin draped with a Union Flag containing machine guns and other lethal weapons.

On another occasion shortly after a similar exercise at Newton Abbot, where we were informed the Mayor had surrendered the town and collaborated with the enemy, an exercise was staged at Dartmouth. Our Mayor, being determined that there should be no similar occurrence, evaded capture by hiding together with the City Fathers and the Captain's wife, who was the W.V. S. Liaison Officer, under a bridge while the enemy went over it. The sight of this distinguished party must have been worth seeing but they lived to fight another day. The last full scale exercise was held in bitter weather early in 1942 and went on for 24 hours. It was so cold that the water froze in the Cadets' water bottles, and two regular soldiers died of exposure.' (*Britannia Magazine*, Easter 1947, p.8).

Two of the steamers on the River Dart were requisitioned in case of invasion and kept fully stocked with provisions to evacuate the Junior College up river if necessary, thus denying the invading forces of four year's supply of future officers. This threat was also taken seriously by the Admiralty, a memorandum dated 14th April 1942 from their Lordships to the Captain of the College informed him of alternative accommodation arrangements for the cadets should the need arise. It stated that the cadets and their teaching and domestic staff would be sent as follows: seventy-two to Shrewsbury School, seventy-two to St Chad's College, Denstone, Staffordshire, ninety to King William's College, Castletown, Isle of Man, and thirty-six to Trent College, Long Eaton Derbyshire. This amounted to 270 cadets, that is six full terms of forty-five. However, when the College was bombed, only five months after the issue of the above memorandum, the plan was not executed, perhaps because the school terms had already started and it would have caused too much disruption.

The Captain issued guidance to deal with the threat of daylight air raids, a copy of which still exists in the College Archive, as reproduced below.

PROPOSED TEMPORARY ORDERS TO BE BROUGHT INTO FORCE CONSEQUENT ON LOW FLYING DAYLIGHT BOMBING

1. Cadets are always to carry Steel Helmets when in the College building and grounds.
2. Divisions are to be cut as short as possible not more than 2 terms are to be fallen in together.
3. Meals – Dartmouth cadets and Special Entry cadets are to mess at different times in the cadets mess to avoid too large an assembly of cadets.
4. Church – Divine Service in the Chapel is to be conducted as at present with two services, Dartmouth Cadets and Special Entry Cadets at separate services.
5. Class Rooms – In the event of a snap raid cadets should take cover under the desks and wear steel helmets.
   No cadets are to take cover near a door or window.

The statue of King George V survives with minor damage from the destruction of the Quarterdeck. Photograph by John Barlee.

Officers and masters instructing cadets are requested to carry steel helmets and to wear them as necessary both for an example to the cadets and for their own safety.

6. Living spaces, classrooms, lecture-rooms etc., inhabited by cadets are always to have glass windows and roofs protected on the inboard side by wire.

7. Practice "take cover" for cadets is to be frequently exercised and times taken to improve times to a minimum.

8. It should be impressed on all that for this type of raid there is no warning, if unidentified aircraft are heard approaching, give the order to take cover at once, if it is a false alarm so much the better.

9. If a raid takes place with cadets:-
   a In the playing fields, cadets should dive into the nearest cover and to lie flat, if no cover lie flat and still.
   b If on the river lie still in the bottom of the boat. On no account look up.

10. This type of raid takes place with such speed and suddenness that it is not intended that cadets should take up A.R.P. stations until the raid is over.

11. Steps are being taken to distribute classroom instruction into more widely separated buildings such as the Hostel, the Cadet's Canteen, the Gymnasium.

Any further suggestions by officers and masters will be welcomed NOW.

(Sgd) E.A. Aylmer
CAPTAIN

These orders illustrate how real the threat of air raids was considered to be. Throughout the war there were hundreds of alerts, the majority passing without serious consequences. The area did however suffer attacks on at least nine occasions, inflicting some damage. Bombs also fell in the estuary and on the surrounding countryside. Dartmouth suffered two major raids, the first on 18th September 1942 and the second on 13th February 1943, when the town suffered considerable damage. In the second raid the College building, now abandoned by its staff and students, received a direct hit. The bomb fell on D Block crashing through one of the Hawke dormitories and finally coming to rest in the Common Room, but fortunately failed to explode. That particular bomb now stands outside Ashford House, inscribed 'a present from Adolf Hitler'.

September 1942 had seen the arrival of both a new Captain and a new Headmaster, but neither of them was to be afforded the luxury of a long honeymoon to acquaint himself with the ways of the College. Mr J. W. Stork had taken up his duties about two weeks prior to the beginning of the new term. After only one week in his new position he was in a meeting in the Commander's day cabin discussing

arrangements for the new term. It was the morning of Friday 18th September and after discussing arrangements for the new term the meeting went on to discuss the provisions that had been made for the evacuation of the College, should the need arise. The group was sitting around the table when six Focke-Wulf aeroplanes attacked the College, approaching from the east down Noss Creek, so as to avoid anti-aircraft fire from the town's defences. The first bomb fell only feet away from the meeting, near the junction of O and B Blocks. When the second bomb struck the north-west corner of the Quarterdeck the group was already under the table or behind the settee. The large oak door to the Commander's cabin was blasted into the room smashing a chair that only seconds before had been in use. As the Commander remarked at the time, they had been discussing a most appropriate subject.

But while the occupants of the Commander's cabin had a lucky escape not every one was to be so fortunate. Wren Betty Joan Blake worked in the Confidential Book Office, together with her assistant, Ruth Blake:

'On the morning of September 18th 1942, Ruth and I had to toss a coin as to who should leave the office first to go to the Wren's loo! She won. A few seconds later I heard the all too familiar sound of German aircraft followed shortly by bombs smashing masonry. The office shook. I ran to the quarterdeck, which was adjacent to the classrooms, into a dense cloud of dust, and saw a gaping hole at the north east corner of the area. Because the cadets were away on summer leave the classrooms were empty. The quarterdeck floor was sagging outside the door to the plotting room. I shouted to them not to open the door. I believe they were later able to get out through the front windows. The Wren's loo was beneath the quarterdeck area and I feared for Ruth's safety. When I went down the staircase and saw a mound of stone and rubble against the loo I feared the worst. There was no answer when I called to her. Some College retainers heard me and came out to clear the rubble. At last we heard Ruth's faint voice say, "I am alive but I think the girl in the next cubicle is dead. There is a large stone block balanced across the partition above my head, so how will you open the door to get me out?" Very carefully the men released her. She was lucky to have survived and was surprisingly calm. But, the shock set in later. The girl who died was P.O. Ellen Victoria Whittall. She was crushed by masonry'.

Ellen Whittall was the only fatality from the bombing, but the casualty list could have been much longer. It has been suggested that the raid had been carefully planned to take place the day after the cadets had arrived for the start of term. This might have been the case except that every six years one extra week was added onto the summer leave to even out the terms. Luckily this was one of those years, had it not been, a generation of future naval officers might have been wiped out.

The Captain sent the following memorandum to the Commander-in-Chief Plymouth, detailing the attack and its consequences.

Stokers, nine in number, can be accommodated in North Wing attics.

Hospital has not yet been found, possibilities:–

1. Saighton Grange.
2. Boldsworth Castle
3. Build for R.N.C.

W.R.N.S accommodation will be in Huts. The Superintendent of W.R.N.S. and S.C.E. will arrange site and layout.

It can be seen from the above that much work remained to be done to prepare Eaton Hall for the arrival of not only the cadets but also the W.R.N.S. There was a telephone switchboard but only two outside lines and fourteen internal extensions, though at the time no one actually knew where these were located. A larger switchboard was obviously necessary and the work put in hand. Fourteen extra huts were to be built in addition to the six already

The Captain and an unknown Admiral take the salute at the march past at what appears to be a passing-out parade in front of Eaton Hall.

The Hawke Term huts add a regimented dimension to the formal gardens of the Eaton Estate.

A group of WRNS Officers mix with other members of the College staff, including on the left, the legendary Miss Bulla.

there. These would be the gunrooms, classrooms, sleeping huts and washing blocks. The existing sleeping huts were to be modified by putting in fitments for basins and an Elsan, no running water or drains were to be provided.

Once the accommodation had been taken care of, the training needs of the cadets also had to be considered. While at Dartmouth the close proximity of the River Dart for all river activities and seamanship training could be taken for granted. The fact that Eaton Hall stood beside the lower reaches of the River Dee, which was fairly wide and not too swiftly flowing, was therefore a major consideration in the choice of the site. Negotiations were made with the local boatman at Eaton, a Mr Probyn, who had been hiring out boats. He agreed to take the position of Head Boatman and gave up his business putting his boat shed, landing pontoon and bank moorings at the College's disposal. The site was not ideal, being liable to flooding in the winter, but it would offer boat training for the cadets, and so was made ready to receive the boats from Dartmouth in early 1943.

Formality meets the formal as divisions take place in the grounds of Eaton Hall. The group in the lower left-hand corner are WRNS personnel on administrative duties.

Naval additions, including the bell from the battleship HMS Britannia *and the College's ensign, to the impressive entrance hall of the Duke of Westminster's residence.*

The move north to Cheshire required a co-ordinated effort. The Great Western Railway, just as in the First World War, competently and without fuss moved everything needed. The boats were taken either entirely by rail or to Ellesmere Port from where they were moved via the Manchester Ship and the Shropshire Union Canals to the River Dee. However, the official move did not include 'Britannia V', the cow belonging to the Captain's wife, Mrs Aylmer. At her own expense she hired the GWR to take the cow to Chester Station, where she met the train and then proceeded to walk her bovine pet to the Hall at Eaton. The move to Eaton Hall was not completed until late January 1943. The following from the Captain signalled the official commissioning.

MEMORANDUM
The Royal Naval College has officially commissioned as from to-day, 1st February, 1943.

From this date it will be known as HMS *Britannia* (Royal Naval College, Eaton.)

The establishment is at all times to be referred to as the Royal Naval College and not as Eaton Hall, or any other name.

E. A. AYLMER
CAPTAIN

A stately home Eaton Hall may have been, but on arrival the cadets were to encounter a rather depressing place, with the grounds flooded and the inevitable mess left by the workmen who had undertaken the alterations. The accommodation was largely in huts and the washing and toilet facilities were a far cry from those at

Sketch of Eaton Hall by a cadet, from the Blake Line Book of 1946.

Dartmouth that they had known. However, once the floods retreated, the College cleaned and the first of the spring daffodils started to bloom in the grounds the spirits of the cadets appeared to rise, as borne out by a personal message to the Captain from the First Sea Lord after an Inspection by him on 27th June 1943.

TO CAPTAIN E.A. AYLMER, D.S.C, R.N.
FROM FIRST LORD

PLEASE CONVEY TO ALL CONCERNED MY APPRECIATION OF THE ARRANGEMENTS MADE TODAY AND OF THE SMART TURNOUT OF THE CADETS. I WAS MOST FAVOURABLY IMPRESSED BY THE WAY IN WHICH ALL OFFICERS, MASTERS AND CADETS HAVE ADAPTED THEMSELVES TO THEIR NEW SURROUNDINGS AND I FEEL SURE THAT THE GREAT TRADITIONS OF THE ROYAL NAVAL COLLEGE WILL BE FULLY MAINTAINED. THE TASK OF TRANSFERRING THE COLLEGE WAS A HEAVY ONE AND I CONGRATULATE YOU AND THE HEADMASTER ON THE EFFICIENT MANNER IN WHICH IT WAS CARRIED OUT.

Indeed, the cadets and the staff soon settled back into college routine in its new location. While at Dartmouth the cadets had kept 'house' gardens, gardening being one of the more popular hobbies encouraged by the masters. At Eaton Hall the tradition continued and the cadets planted flower gardens in front of their huts and vegetables in plots behind. Vegetables were also grown in what in peacetime had been herbaceous borders in front of the Hall and the produce used to supplement the galley requirement. The Commander detailed parties to tend the gardens, under the supervision of Mr E. T. Warner, one of the retired masters brought back to help out for the duration of the war, a task in which the cadets took great pride. The Duke often used to walk in the gardens of the Hall with his gold–topped tall walking cane, stopping to chat to the cadets.

The Duke was also adapting to his new house guests, becoming a familiar figure to the cadets and the staff at the College. On arrival at the Hall the Commander had instructed assembled cadets that if they saw an old man walking around followed by dachshunds that they were to salute him. The Duke himself did not seem to understand the constraints of the working day, it was not unknown for him to telephone John Barlee, one of the young masters, while he was in a staff meeting to ask for help with a crossword clue. When he was at home he would occasionally invite academic staff and officers to 'coffee and liqueurs', when he would recount his own exploits in the First World War in Russia when he had his own Rolls Royce armoured car troop manned by estate employees.

Ladies they may be, but they are not averse to competing with the men in a game of cricket, the photographer captures them walking to the cricket square.

'I was really lucky to be based at the College – it was a fantastic time for me. I spent all my spare minutes in the college boats based at Sandquay, rowing and sailing. I also belonged to the Naval Base cricket team (ten sailors and me!). We were allowed to use all the college facilities – gym, swimming pool, cricket nets, shoe repair shops, canteen for the base staff, and join sailing boat activities. We would go to the film shows for the cadets, and to their parades and prizegivings. We hardly visited the town, because of the limitless activity at the college'.

As a despatch rider she would take despatches to ships in the harbour as well as to the Commander in Chief Plymouth and to the resident Naval officers at the various bases such as Teignmouth, Brixham, Exmouth, Torbay and to the army bases at Slapton Sands and on Dartmoor. (Freeman, 1994).

What the cadets thought of the arrival of the WRNS is not recorded but an influx of females at the College must have caused some comments amongst them. After the move to Eaton Hall they were billeted in the former cadet's dormitories as Clare Hanscombe recalls in A Wrens-Eye View of Dartmouth.

'We slept in dormitories of about 32 girls. At the foot of each double bunk (two tier) was a four drawer chest of drawers, a mirror behind the bunks, a shelf and a rail on which to hang garments and store suitcases. I would say the average age was about 21–22 years, so you can imagine the fun we had at times. Our dining hall and galley was in a separate and I think temporary buildings close to the Wren's block'.

The importance of the work carried out by the WRNS, in Dartmouth in particular and for the war effort in general cannot be praised too highly, they were an integral and vital part of the war effort. At the end of the war many of the WRNS were demobilised and returned to civilian life, however this mammoth task required a large number of them to be retained to administer it. By June of 1946 the WRNS numbers were down to 15,000 and declining but a Government White Paper in May 1946 on the future of all the Services announced the retention of the Service. In February 1949 the WRNS became a permanent service, separate from but integral with the Royal Navy. The 1950s were a period of consolidation for the Service and permanent training headquarters were established. In July 1974 HRH The Princess Anne became Chief Commandant WRNS and one of her early duties was to take the salute at the final WRNS OTC passing out parade in March of 1976 at The Royal Naval College Greenwich. They had been trained at Greenwich since October 1939, except for short time when the College was evacuated because of bomb damage. Initially this training was a basic two weeks but had been extended over the years to three months.

In September 1976 the first WRNS officer training course arrived at Britannia Royal Naval College, and remained three months (one term) in length. The decision to move to Dartmouth was taken because by this time the training had broadened to encompass wider naval responsibilities and there was a limit as to what could be achieved when isolated from the main officer training establishment. A separate division was set for them, Talbot Division, named after Mary Talbot (Director of WRNS 1973-76). This one term pattern of training remained until in January 1992 the first totally integrated intake of women into the Royal Navy began.

The Women's Royal Naval Service thus ceased to exist, those women entering the Navy now undertaking exactly the same training as their male counterparts. They hold the same ranks or rates, go to sea, are promoted or advanced in open competition, paid the same salary and most of all are subject to the same code of discipline and conditions of service. Gone were the blue stripes of the WRNS, officers now wearing gold as the men had done before them. All roles are now open to them except service in submarines.

Her Royal Highness The Princess Anne in her uniform as the Chief Commandant of WRNS. The blue braid was replaced with gold upon full integration in 1990.

that HM King would be broadcasting to the Empire and the United States of America at nine o'clock and so Exmouth did their prep at 1945–2030 so that we could listen to the speech in pyjamas.'

The College was to remain in its northern home throughout the war, as only makeshift repairs to make the structure safe were undertaken at Dartmouth. It was at Eaton, therefore that the end of the war was celebrated, as recalled in the 'Blake' Division Line Book of 1945:

'The Term began on the 11th May, just as everyone was recovering from the "VE-Day" celebrations. On the first Sunday of term there was a Victory Parade through Chester, to which Terms 11, 10, 9 and some of the Ships Company were invited. As the only representatives of the Royal Navy, we marched at the head of the procession led by our own Marine Band, which shared the task of providing the music with the A.T.C. Band. After marching past the G.O.C. Western Command we completed a two-mile round course and back to our buses in Frodsham Street. Although there was a nasty moment just before the Saluting Base, when the Cheshire Regiment Band broke into the wrong tune, but all went well, and we acquitted ourselves quite well, especially as we had no marching practice for a month.'

Once again the cadet's training had come to the fore, a training that had helped to sustain them and their predecessors throughout the darkest days of the war.

Although a year was to pass before the College could return to Dartmouth, the College buildings had been far from dormant throughout the war. As the staff and students of the Royal Naval College had been carrying on with their routine in their alternative surroundings, so the buildings they had left behind, initially known as HMS *Dartmouth III*, were to take on a new role, which would ensure they continued to play a very active part in the Allied war effort. In this role the building did not require restoration after the bomb damage so only temporary repairs to make the building safe were carried out, the major repair work being carried out between September 1945 to August 1946. Initially the College, re-named HMS *Effingham* in July 1943, was taken over by Combined Operations, for the training of Royal Marines in the art of amphibious warfare. Then on 27th December 1943, having already been in the area for a month, the Americans arrived to take over the College on behalf of the US Naval Advanced Amphibious Base (USNAAB). USNAAB was just one of the many Allied bases to be used along the south coast for training and preparations in the run up to the D-Day invasion of Europe in June 1944. American forces stationed throughout Devon and Cornwall were known as *U Force*, being destined to land on Utah Beach on the Cherbourg peninsula, which closely resembled the South Devon coast.

First impressions of the College for the American forces were not good. An official American report on USNAAB, recalls that plumbing, heating and other comfort-giving facilities appeared to have been neglected, in contrast to the customs and traditions of the Royal Navy, which had been vigorously maintained. Indeed, one RN Commander who stayed on after the change over was horrified to see the Quarterdeck become a storage room for boxes of cigarettes and worse, to witness a match being struck on the base of the statue of George V to light an American cigar (Freeman 1996, p.10). For the newly arrived Americans, however, the priority was to make the College liveable. Space was limited, with classrooms having to be transformed into living quarters. Housekeeping materials, beds and toilet paper were all at a premium, the previous owners having being careful not to leave anything behind, each Royal Marine taking with him a light bulb in addition to the rest of his kit.

As D-Day approached USNAAB became increasingly busy, its principal task being the repair of ships and landing craft for the preparation and execution of the invasion. By the beginning of 1944 over 4000 USN personnel were billeted in the Dartmouth area, along with various army units, British liaison groups, war correspondents, high ranking army and navy officials and members of observation tours. The College was filled to capacity and a tent city was set up in the College grounds. Finally, on 1st June US troops and their equipment were loaded on to their transport craft for the last time and set sail on June 4th, taking shelter in Weymouth Bay on the 5th until the storm that swept the English Channel had abated, before reaching Normandy on the 6th June.

For the next few months USNAAB was to be fully occupied repairing landing craft but as the Allied forces advanced into France so its importance began to decline. It was too far west to be used to supply forces in France or receive casualties. As a final act, on 29th April 1945, as the war in Europe was drawing to a close, the St. Columba Window was presented to the College Chapel on behalf of members of the United States Navy resident at the Royal Naval College. Commodore Korns USN, who was Commander of the Amphibious Base, United Kingdom made the presentation. In making the gift Commodore Korns acknowledged that while at the College he and his men had constantly striven to preserve the College and its traditions, and that he had personally derived much inspiration from the use of the chapel. Captain Warner accepted the gift on behalf of the College and said that it would be appreciated throughout the Service, as it expressed the deep feelings of friendship that existed between the United States Navy and the Royal Navy. Moreover, after their return to Dartmouth, this handsome gift would help them to recall the critical contribution that sea power had made to enable the Allied armies to invade France and precipitate the liberation of Europe.

Combined Operations during Sunday divisions at HMS Effingham *in 1943. The impact of the war is evident with the figurehead of* Britannia *having been painted to camouflage her and the barbed wire around the parade ground to guard against attack.*

*The still war-scarred College as United States Naval
Advanced Amphibious Base in 1944.*

Education 1945-2005

The end of the Second World War in 1945 heralded the beginning of a new era, one in which the role and position of Britain, the Royal Navy and Dartmouth would all be fundamentally challenged and changed. As Paul Kennedy observes in charting *The Rise and Fall of British Naval Mastery,* with the end of the war, long-term trends, 'the relative weakening of the British economy, the rise of the super-powers, the disintegration of the European empires, the decline of sea power in its classical form *vis-à-vis* land and air power, the growing public demand for increased domestic rather than foreign expenditure - now combined to overwhelm a British naval mastery that had long been in question.' (Kennedy 1983, p. 383). The combination of the decline of British power and the change in society, reflected in the administration of the post-war Socialist government and its successors, was to have a profound effect on the way in which appropriate officer training would be conducted at Dartmouth. Between 1945 and 1960 there were to be no less than five fundamental reviews of the Naval College, including its transformation from public school to naval academy. In contrast to the first forty years of relative stability, the latter sixty years in the life of Britannia Royal Naval College have been permeated by change, culminating in some of the most fundamental reforms to the structure and delivery of training and education at Dartmouth as the College approached its centenary.

Return from Eaton Hall and the Beginning of an Era of Change

Following the bombing of the College in September 1942, only patch-work repairs had been possible, given the wartime shortages of labour and material. It was, therefore, to be another year after the end of the war before the College was fit for cadets and staff to return. In addition to the repair work a number of improvements were made to extend the library and science laboratories; fluorescent lighting, an automatic telephone system and a loud-speaker system were installed. A competition was held by the Captain to find a new design to replace the electroliers that had been destroyed along with the quarterdeck roof and work began on a new block (F-block) to provide extra classrooms for the new additions to the curriculum - music and art. Nevertheless, on the College's return there were too many cadets to be catered for altogether, necessitating the conversion of staff quarters into a dining room with a separate servery on a different floor to the galley. Two sittings were required for breakfast, dinner (mid-day) and supper and serving staff had to be organised into watches to cope.

The Royal Naval College returned to Dartmouth in September 1946. Officers and cadet captains had joined in advance to reconnoitre and draw up plans, which were posted up to indicate to staff and students alike where they were in their strange new surroundings. Meanwhile scores of workmen finished off their refurbishment work, restoring the building to its former glory, as a master at the time observed; 'the gallery of the Quarter-deck had been restored so well that it was hard to see the join between the old and the new' (Hughes p.158). Despite these upheavals College life continued much as it had at Eaton, including wartime additions such as visits from guest lecturers. In the winter of 1947 one such lecture was given by Viscount Mountbatten of Burma who spoke about the difficulties of jungle warfare and joint and combined operations. At the end Mountbatten made a presentation to the College of two Japanese swords, one of which is still displayed on the wall outside the quarterdeck. Other visitors that year included the King and Queen. On inspecting the statue of George V on the quarterdeck His Majesty noticed it had been damaged during the bombing and expressed the wish that it should not be restored but remain, as it does, a memorial.

However, while continuity reigned at Dartmouth the seeds of reform were already being sown. In July 1945 the 'Noble Committee on Entry into the Royal Naval College, Dartmouth,'(ADM 1/17293) was set up to consider whether there were grounds to improve the current system. Since 1941 there had been two modes of entry for boys aged thirteen, when a scholarship scheme was introduced to encourage boys from grant-aided secondary schools through a system of reduced fees for those from families on lower incomes. There were thus two systems of entry based on the Common Entrance Examination for Public Schools. For the old or 'ordinary cadet' system a pass mark of 55% followed by an interview to determine intelligence, capability, character and personality were required. For the 'scholarship cadets' a pass mark of 65% and a more straight-forward suitability interview was required. However, as the Noble Committee was to report in 1946, while the ordinary entry continued to satisfy the requirements for successful naval cadets the scholarship system had introduced a 'small tail of weak candidates' into the system. Of even greater concern, however, was the steady decline in numbers competing for both entries, a decline felt to be in excess of a reaction against a service career following a major war or even the reduced birth rate of the 1930s. The findings of the Committee therefore concluded that the selection process for both forms of entry should be more rigorous and that a publicity programme should be initiated by the Admiralty, to appeal particularly to the boys and headmasters of grant-aided grammar schools. However, it also recognised that a 'radical transformation in national education is about to take place,' and that consequently it was 'difficult to see how the Royal Naval College in its present form can hope to conform with such a national system.'

That there should be a further investigation into the system of entry to Dartmouth was therefore inevitable, although as he wrote prior to its announcement in the House of Commons in May 1947, Prime Minister Atlee was at pains to make 'clear to the country that the changes I am making do not result from any dissatisfaction with the past.' As he went on to tell the House;

> 'It cannot be too strongly emphasised that we have every reason to be satisfied with the quality of the naval officer produced by the entry of boys at about 13 years of age and the subsequent

education at Dartmouth. The Royal Navy can justly claim that its officers have stood the supreme test of war . . . The best tribute to Dartmouth is the distinction with which the product has served the country.' (ADM 1/20918)

The need for change, it was emphasised, was brought about as a result of changes in the system of national education that had taken place over the past forty years. Moreover, 'inevitably, entry was the privilege of boys whose parents were able to afford to send their children to preparatory schools,' where the natural age of advancement was thirteen – an important consideration for the Socialist government as it strove towards social equality in education. The new system was announced in January 1948, its twin objectives to ensure that no boy should be disqualified from a career as a naval officer on the basis of social status, financial situation or schooling, while providing the Navy with officers of the highest academic standards, character and leadership qualities. This was to be achieved in dramatic fashion. In consultation with the Admiralty and Ministry of Education, together with opinions from other educational authorities and eminent Naval Officers, it was decided the thirteen year old entry would to be phased out over the next two years, the last such entry joining in May 1949. In its place there would be three entries per year to the Executive, Engineering and Supply Branches at the age of sixteen to sixteen years and four months old, the first joining Dartmouth in September 1948. Tuition and boarding fees were abolished and the cost of uniforms would be subsidised when necessary. The entrance exam would be devised so as not to disadvantage boys from any particular sort of school, and candidates would also undergo tests of intelligence, aptitude, character and personality before a board consisting of naval officers, a psychologist, a representative from the state system of education and a headmaster on rotation from the state and public school systems. The Special Entry at eighteen years of age was to continue, with the ultimate aim of recruiting twenty-five per cent of commissioned officers by promotion from the lower deck and of the remainder half each from the sixteen and eighteen year old entry (Statement to the House of Commons, 28/1/1948, ADM 1/22690).

By democratising the entry it was hoped that the Royal Navy would be able to continue to recruit the best officers from a decreasing available population, in terms of numbers and inclination, while shaking off any allegations of anachronistic snobbery. However, the sixteen-year-old entry was by no means universally acclaimed and also raised questions about the continuing suitability of Aston Webb's College for its task. Consequently, in March 1949 a committee was appointed to assess the best use of the accommodation available at Dartmouth.

The problem, as reported by the 'Dartmouth Accommodation Committee' (ADM 1/21773) in July 1950, was that the raising of the age of entry to Dartmouth would lead to a reduction in the number

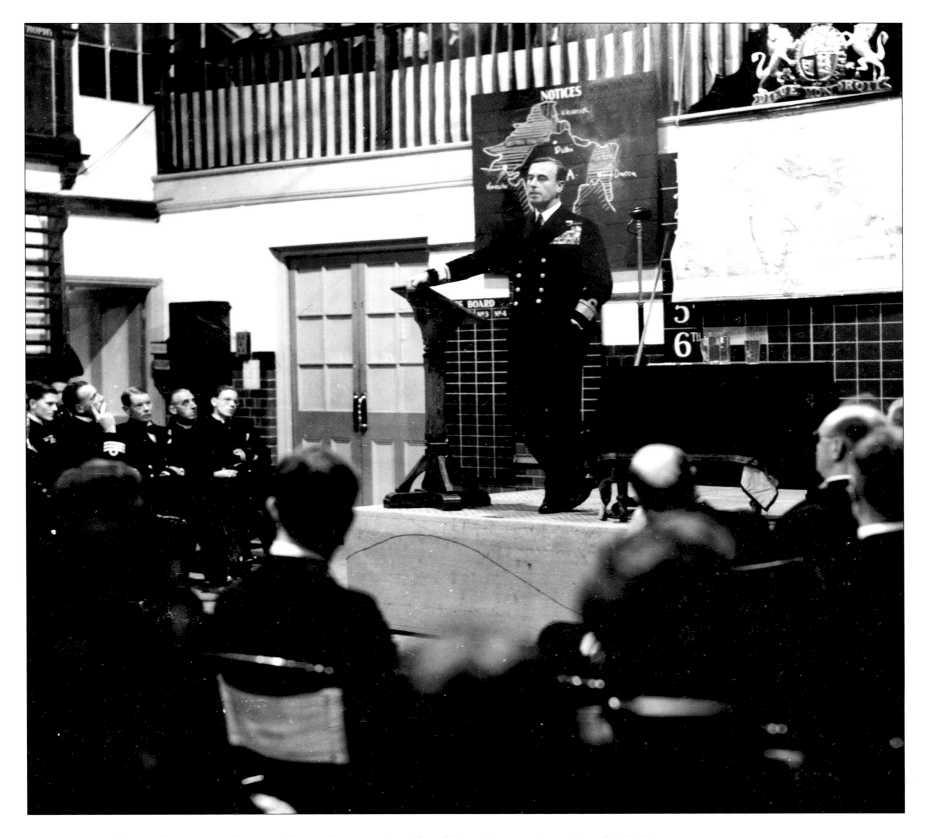

Viscount Mountbatten of Burma speaking to cadets in the gymnasium about his wartime experiences in early 1947.

of cadets from 500 to 280. Overhead costs, however, would not decline as buildings and facilities still had to be maintained. The net result was that whereas in 1939 the average cost per cadet was £130, by 1950 it had risen to £500 and was estimated to increase to £800 by 1953. Meanwhile accommodation itself was also becoming available, with a surplus of boarding school accommodation in the main building for 220 boys, sleeping and messroom space for a hundred in the old ship company's block, and spare capacity for fifty-six in sick quarters (as sixteen year old boys suffered less sickness that thirteen year olds). A number of suggestions for using this spare capacity were suggested, including: the transfer of the Upper Yardmen's College and Admiralty Interview Board from HMS *Hawke* at Exbury; making Dartmouth a junior naval university, with Greenwich as the senior, through the transfer of the Sub-Lieutenants' General Education and War Course from Greenwich; or turning the College into a boarding school providing a normal course of education, with a naval bias. Of these suggestions only the first two were finally recommended. The proposal to move the Sub-Lieutenants' course was ruled out, partly due to a lack of accommodation and appropriately qualified staff, but also because it was felt that, 'it would be a psychological mistake to send Sub-Lieutenants back to the school atmosphere of Dartmouth, with its strict and almost monastic discipline . . .' (Ibid.). The suggestion to turn the College into a boarding school was not, however, ruled out but declared to be beyond the remit of the Committee. Nevertheless, it was noted that Naval members of the Committee 'consider the only suitable way to fill Dartmouth would be to adopt the proposal to convert the College into a boarding school.'(Ibid.). Finally it was agreed that unless means could be found to make further economies and utilise all available capacity, that 'the Admiralty may have to move the training of naval cadets from Dartmouth to a smaller and cheaper establishment.' (Ibid.).

Inevitably, therefore, the system that had been introduced in 1948 was soon under review. In July 1951 a report was commissioned into the sixteen-year-old entry and the quality of candidates from secondary grammar schools (ADM 1/22463). The findings were not encouraging, concluding that the best grammar school boys were simply not applying. As a result boys from independent schools continued to perform better than their state school counter parts in competing for places at Dartmouth.[1] Clearly it was far too soon after the introduction of the sixteen-year-old entry to assess its success in producing naval officers of the highest quality. However, it was already clear that it was failing to achieve the supposedly secondary objective of enabling equal opportunities for boys from all backgrounds.

1 For example, between May 1949 and February 1951, 449 boys from independent schools sat the entrance exam, of whom 144 passed. Of those, 106 passed the Admiralty Interview Board (AIB) and 97 were accepted. In contrast, 1366 grammar school boys sat the exam, of whom just 311 passed the exam and 96 passed the AIB, with 90 candidates finally being accepted.

Instruction in the classroom.

Thus in July 1952 a 'Committee on Cadet Entry' was appointed, under the chairmanship of the Judge Advocate of the Fleet, the Honourable Ewen Montagu. This time, however, the findings of the Committee were to be made public so as to encourage the widest possible debate. The Montagu Committee reported in May 1953 in a blaze of publicity, focused upon accusations of 'snobbery' in the selection process. These allegations had been fuelled by press reporting, such as a 1952 report in the *Daily Express*, following a top grammar school boy who had passed the written exam four times but each time had been rejected by the interview board. Indeed, the report recognised that if they passed the written exam boys from a public school stood a sixty-eight per cent chance of success in the oral examination, compared to a twenty-eight per cent chance for a grammar school boy. Despite having been designed to catch boys leaving school on completion of their general certificate of education, school-masters in public[2] and grammar schools were reluctant to lose their best pupils, who could be primed for university. Public school boys therefore continued to take the

2 The Headmaster of Eton wrote a letter to *The Times*, criticising the sixteen-year-old entry (7/7/1953).

After hours: prep and a game of cards

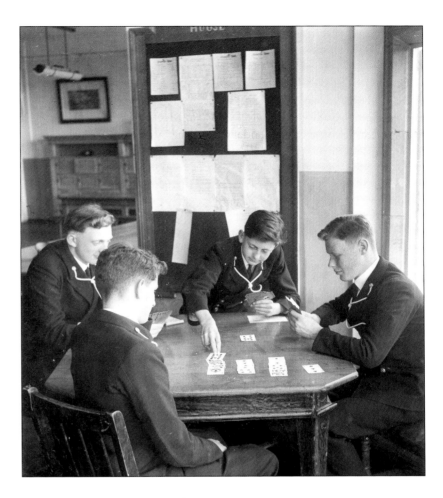

member of the Montagu Committee produced his own minority report, recommending the eventual move to an all eighteen entry to reflect the growing trend in national education. In November 1953, the government decided to accept Barraclough's report, abolishing the thirteen and sixteen year old entries and the old Special Entry within the next two years. The overriding objective, Parliament was told was; 'to establish a system of Cadet entry into the Royal Navy which not only gives the Navy adequate numbers of cadets of the required standard but conforms beyond dispute with the general trend of educational policy and is entirely beyond the field of controversy.' (ADM 1/30995) The Montagu Report could not, therefore, be accepted on the basis of the conditions it had placed upon itself, i.e. that its findings should be acceptable to public and educational opinion. As First Lord of the Admiralty, J.P.L. Thomas, wrote to Lord Mountbatten (ADM 1/30995):

> 'I hope you are not too disappointed about the cadet entry decision. There was really no alternative and the Sea Lords all agreed that they did not wish to return to the 13 entry with all the conditions attached to it by the Montagu Report; and everybody was agreed that the 16 entry was producing unfortunate results. It was therefore felt that the bravest thing to

> do was to go right out for 17 – 19 . . .
> 'I really believe that we have now placed cadet entry above party politics and I hear from Jim Callaghan that we have taken a decision which no political party would wish to upset.'

The fact that reform of the Royal Naval College attracted so much public debate and involved personalities from the Prime Minister down, is testament to the regard in which the Royal Navy was held in the aftermath of the Second World War. Nevertheless, the system of naval education established under Fisher, revolutionary in its own time, had inevitably succumbed to what today would be termed political correctness. The armed forces have long claimed to reflect the society they serve; in 1950s Britain this was a society in which age-long class barriers were finally being broken, in a new era of equality of opportunity. Simultaneously, the very rationale behind Britain's Navy was also being eroded, the Empire that it had served was contracting and the future wars that it might fight looked like being very short and extremely destructive in the new atomic age. Against such a background of change within Britain and Britain's place in the world it was therefore inevitable that an institution such as Dartmouth would need to reform if it was to survive into its second half century.

From Public School to Training Establishment

In January 1954, the Committee on Officer Structure and Training (COST) was appointed under the chairmanship of Vice Admiral Sir Aubrey Mansergh. Its remit was to report on the officer structure of the future, but owing to its urgency the first matter to be investigated was the initial training scheme of young Naval Officers, both to meet the new conditions and reflect scientific and technological advances. In accordance with the Committee's recommendations three working groups were set up: 'A' to work out the curriculum and syllabus for the new scheme and the staff required; 'B' to consider the composition of the Training Squadron; and 'C' to consider the necessary works and buildings at Dartmouth. The length of the course would be seven, thirteen-week terms, divided into three phases. The first phase consisted of two terms of naval training and academic levelling, during the second phase cadets spent one term in the Dartmouth Training Squadron (DTS) learning about life at sea[3], after which they were promoted to midshipmen. The third phase consisted of four terms academic and professional training interspersed with short periods with the DTS and a visit to a naval air station.

It was recognised that as the students would be young men who had left school it was proper to reduce the amount of regimentation that had permeated the old system, while maintaining high levels of discipline and paying the greatest attention to training in leadership. Students would be encouraged to think for themselves, work for themselves and use their leisure time profitably. Inevitably, this would require a period of adjustment for the staff, even for the inimitable Miss Bulla, who prescribed extra milk rations to one Cadet (later Captain) Wixon when he appeared somewhat pale at breakfast, unaware that he had spent the previous evening at the Floating Bridge public house.

On the academic side the tutorial system would be adopted where possible, time being divided between lectures, private study and tutorial periods consisting of two or three students and a lecturer. It was assumed that new entrants would be of or above the necessary intellectual level but would have studied a wide variety of subjects. Everyone would therefore have to be brought up to a minimum standard in mathematics and science in addition to naval history and modern languages where possible. In professional training the emphasis would be on teaching principles that could be built upon as a foundation at a later date, without the need for separate specialist training, allowing all cadets to learn about each other's jobs[4]. This theoretical work would then be put into practice during periods at sea.

One of the most immediate implications of introducing a new system concerned the future of the civilian masters. As mentioned above, despite their obvious qualifications to advise on the subject of naval education, the Dartmouth academics had been largely

The front cover from the Britannia Magazine, *midsummer 1949. The first magazine was published in 1884. Its aims were to provide a vehicle for cadets and staff to voice their opinions and a record of sporting and other notable events. It is the source of much valuable material for the researcher and there are some very talented pieces of artwork within its pages, but most importantly it gives an often humorous, sometimes sad, but unique insight into College life over the past one hundred years.*

3 The DTS consisted of three Type 15 anti-submarine frigates and two minesweepers: HMS *Vigilant, Venus, Carron, Jewel* and *Acute.*
4 In 1954 the distinctive colours for the various branches in the RN were abolished and in 1956, in line with COST and the introduction of the 'General List', the supplementary (E), (S) and (L) to the rank of Engineer, Supply and Electrical Officers were removed as these officers were now to have common entry and training with Seamen Officers (no longer called Executive).

The reward for all that practice; dancing with a Rear Admiral!

overlooked in the public debate over their future. It was acknowledged in the House of Commons on 25th November 1953 that some of the masters, 'have devoted most of their lives to the education of naval cadets.' However, it was not possible 'to speak about their prospects of further employment after Dartmouth ceases to be concerned with cadets of school age.' (ADM 1/30995). Before the official announcement had been made Second Master G. Ghey had written to the Admiralty, on behalf of all the masters, pledging their collective loyalty but asking in return for some security of tenure. Nevertheless, when the announcement was finally made, as the Captain of the College, W.S. Crawford noted, it 'naturally left the Masters completely in the air.' (BRNC Archive). Ultimately, however, eighteen of the twenty-four masters on the staff in 1954, survived the changes to 1956 and beyond. The post of Headmaster became Director of Studies[5], with an Assistant Director of Studies, Heads of Departments (Science, Mathematics, Modern Languages and History and English – as under the old system), Senior Lecturers and Junior Lecturers. Under this new structure, based upon the lecturer system at Sandhurst, the academics became Civil Servants and full members of the Wardroom Mess. Overall the new scheme saw an increase in both academic and naval staff, which together with the increased number of cadets, who being older required more personal space, led to extensive building works to adapt and expand the College buildings.[6]

As Davies and Grove commented in their history of the College's first seventy-five years; 'the conversion to tertiary college was in principle more radical than the changes of 1905.' (1980, p.20). The rise in age of entry to eighteen meant not merely changes in curriculum and teaching methods but denied to the Navy the

opportunity to mould its future officers at a younger, more impressionable age, as Captain Pack observed: 'There were still those who argued that the best training ground was in a ship at sea, and the younger they went to sea the more quickly would cadets become able naval officers.' Nevertheless, it was recognised that as ships became technologically more complex all officers would require a sound understanding of their working; 'with the onset of the technological age there is an inherent conflict between the requirement for deeper professional study and the wish to learn on the job.' And in an uncanny prediction for the future; 'The best training scheme can only be a compromise . . . The result is that we encounter a recommended shake-up every five years instead of the fifty envisaged half a century ago.' (1966, p.265).

Indeed, the new system was barely up and running before yet another review was announced, due in part to the recommendation in COST, which set-up the 'General List' (GL) of officers from various specialisations. A committee was appointed in April 1958, under the chairmanship of Sir Keith Murray, Chairman of the University Grants Committee. The Committee found two serious shortcomings in the existing system:

'Firstly, the standard of entry of most of those who are now going to Dartmouth appears to us to be too low to meet either the demands made upon them by the existing syllabus or the future needs of the Navy. Secondly, the phasing of the present scheme seems to us to make impossible achievement of the full development, within the time limits imposed, of those qualities of character which a naval officer must possess.' (BRNC Archive)

While it was recognised that the COST system had yet to produce any sub-lieutenants for the fleet an immediate review of both the existing method of entry and training programme were considered essential. Ideally the Committee was, 'convinced that the 13 year old entry, if it could be reintroduced, would be the best for the Navy,' but it was also appreciated, 'that for political and social reasons it is impossible to put back the clock' (BRNC Archive). The eighteen-year-old entry was to remain but to attain a higher quality of cadet a minimum of two 'A' Levels was required, preferably including mathematics and physics. For the first year the emphasis was on developing leadership qualities. The first term of basic naval training would smooth the transition from civilian to service life; the second term would be spent in the DTS acclimatising to life at sea; the third term of introductory naval

5 The last to fill the post of Headmaster and first Director of Studies was J.W. Stork CB, CBE, MA. Mr Stork had arrived at Dartmouth as Headmaster just two weeks before the College was bombed in September 1942. He had then overseen the removal of the College up to Eaton Hall and back again. After the war he oversaw the end of the 13-year-old entry, the introduction and abolition of the 16-year-old entry, and finally the end of Dartmouth's days as a school with the introduction of the all 18-year-old entry.
6 See Chapter 2 on Architecture.

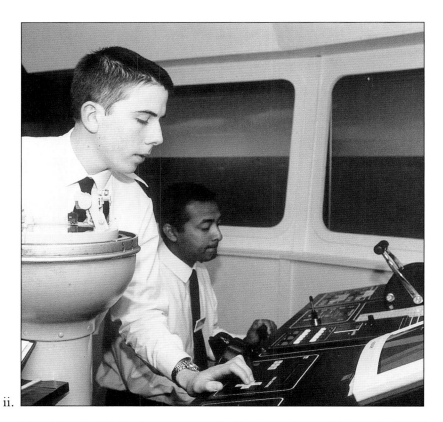

courses would give cadets preliminary appreciation of the functions performed by naval officers, together with basic instruction in navigation and naval history, discipline and physical training. The whole of the second year would be spent at sea as midshipmen, before returning to Dartmouth as acting sub-lieutenants for a year of academics. The only exception from this pattern was for engineers, who went to the Royal Naval Engineering College, Manadon for two years on returning from sea. The remainder at Dartmouth received academic courses of first-year degree level, as the Murray Committee acknowledged:

> 'Apart from the argument that the Navy has no right to good calibre minds that it is not prepared to educate further, it is called for because without it the subsequent professional and sub-specialist training can never have full value.' (BRNC Archive)

In addition to mathematics, science and engineering the curriculum included English, foreign languages, social studies (i.e. the study of contemporary society, in which the Navy works and from which it draws its personnel) and Naval History – considered to be 'important in its own sake.' That Dartmouth should remain the location for the new scheme was supported by the Committee, on the basis that, 'Naval tradition, the buildings, the river, and the general training facilities all provide strong arguments for keeping Dartmouth as the central naval officer training establishment.' (BRNC Archive)

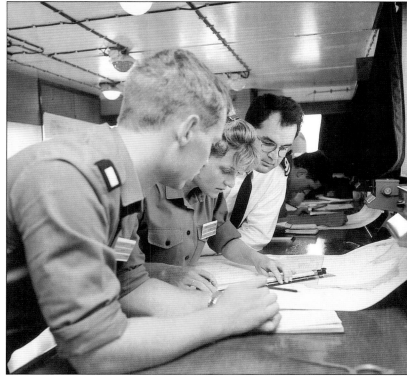

Navigation training. i. HMS Sealark, *the bridge trainer (simulator). ii. Bridge trainer in use by Young Officers. iii. Practical navigation training at sea.*

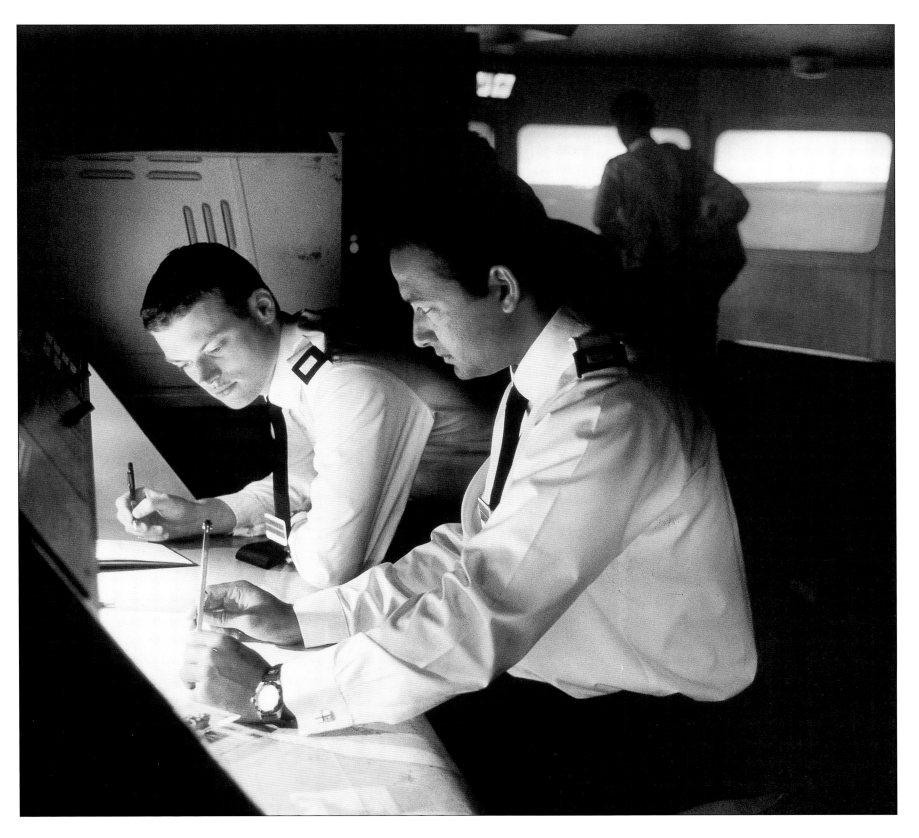

Navigation training. Bridge trainer in use by Young Officers.

The River

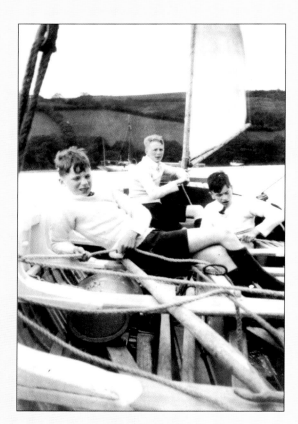

*O*ne of Dartmouth's greatest assets is the sheltered harbour that is offered by the estuary of the River Dart. This was the primary reason for the mooring of Britannia and Hindostan in the river in the 1860s and it has always offered a safe haven for the many varied waterborne activities. The workshops at Sandquay not only provided the engineering workshops for the College, so vital to the success of the Selborne Scheme, but also the skilled workforce who maintained and built many of the smaller craft.

Left and below: Cadets enjoying the River in the 1930s.

Seamanship instruction on the previous training vessel *Hindostan* and a picket boat.

Blowing the cobwebs away in a RIB (rigid inflatable boat).

Dinghy sailing in the College Bosun craft.   Safety first!

After the storm: picket boats alongside at Sandquay.

Sail Past in College motor-whalers, followed by an STC (sail training craft).

Hindostan, old and new.

Aerial view of the Sandquay workshops, showing the latest *Hindostan* (seamanship training vessel) and other College craft.

i.

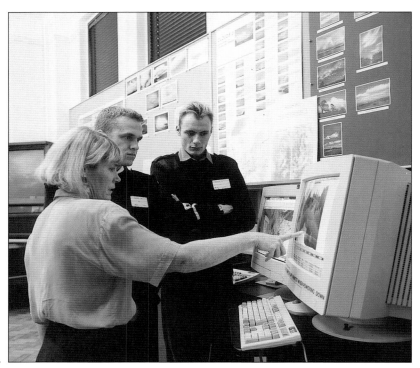

ii.

Academic instruction in;- i. Oceanography; ii. Meteorology.

The first Murray scheme cadets arrived in 1960, however it was becoming evident that the new, higher entry requirements were preventing some boys with suitable character and leadership qualities from joining the service. A 'Supplementary List' (SL) was therefore formed, to complement the 'General List,' firstly for aircrew and then seamen and eventually engineer officers, requiring lower entry grades. SL cadets spent two terms of academic and professional training at Dartmouth before going on to flying training, DTS or Manadon respectively. Other courses were also starting to arrive. The Upper Yardmen Course, for officers promoted from the ranks arrived from HMS *Temeraire* in 1960, taking up residence in what had been the hospital until 1958, when the Admiralty Interview Board used it for a short time. The course lasted two years before they went to sea as midshipmen. In 1962 a special course for 'New Commonwealth' and foreign officers was offered as an alternative to the RN academic course for those that were sufficiently qualified. By 1967 a specific package had been developed for all 'Internationals', with a third term of academics followed by an 'International Senior Term' for more advanced study.

Despite all the efforts to transform naval education after 1945, to make it socially inclusive and more appealing as a career to intellectually gifted school leavers, by the mid-1960s Dartmouth was once again suffering as a result of changing patterns in national education. The 1960s were to see a major expansion in higher education, thus potentially denying the navy and other armed services of its best potential officers as they chose to go to university instead. In 1963 five cadets were nominated to go to university instead of the third year at Dartmouth. A year later the first of what were to become known as the 'Direct Graduate Entry,' (DGE) arrived. In 1965 the 'University Cadet Entry' (UCE) scheme was established, whereby the Navy would sponsor school leavers with university places. On graduation UCEs would go to Dartmouth for professional training and a course in technical subjects for arts graduates. While once again allowing Dartmouth to conform with national trends, the introduction of graduates into the College had the potential to undermine the tradition of unquestioning obedience expected from cadets. The contrast was summed up in the *Britannia Magazine* of Christmas 1964 (p.13):

> 'Traditionally there appears to be a feeling of antagonism between the services and the Universities: this is a mixture of mutual mistrust and jealousy, giving rise to secondary feelings of disdain. The young officer regards the undergraduate as scruffy, while the undergraduate regards the young officer as being incapable of thinking for himself . . . prepared to obey orders without thought.'

The Murray Scheme was finally superseded in 1972 by the 'Naval College Entry' scheme. Under the revised system new entrants would undertake a period of 'Naval General Training,' in professional and character and leadership courses. One term would be spent at iii.

iv.

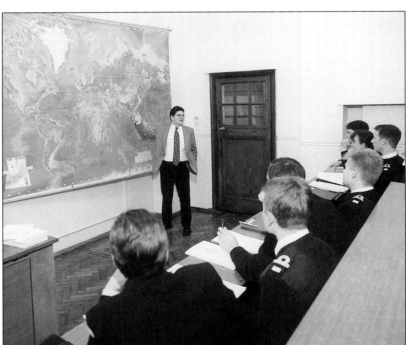

v.

the College, the second on the Dartmouth Training Ship, which replaced the squadron.[7] After that engineers would go to RNEC Manadon or the University of Cambridge and some suitably qualified seamen and supply officers without university places would be 'nominated,' to a university. Non-graduates on the General List would go on to do two, later extended to three, terms of academics at Dartmouth, while SL seamen and supply officers did one term. Meanwhile UCEs were encouraged to defer taking up their places at university in order to undertake the Naval General Training course first. In 1974 the first Special Duties Officers (older ratings commissioned from the ranks) arrived from Greenwich to undertake their one-term professional and academic course, as a separate 'St. George's' Division.

It was not just the educational system that was changing in Britain in the 1960s and 1970s. In the spring of 1973 the first female officers to train at Dartmouth arrived, consisting of eight QARNNS sisters who formed the first short introductory course. In 1976 the WRNS moved their entire officer-training course of one term's professional and academic training to Dartmouth from Greenwich, forming a separate 'Talbot' division. As the Royal Naval College entered its seventy-fifth year in 1980 it had undergone numerous changes since its staff and students had returned from their northern exile in 1946. Much of this change had been brought about by necessity, a most fundamental necessity – to continue to supply the Royal Navy with sufficient numbers of suitably qualified and able officers. In the process the College had been transformed from a public school into a training establishment, where the number of

Academic instruction in;- iii. Engineering Science; iv. Modern Languages v. Strategic Studies and International Affairs.

7 The first to act as Dartmouth Training Ships were HMS *Fearless* and *Intrepid*. They were supplemented in 1982 by HMS *Peterel* and *Sandpiper*, and in 1987 by HMS *Fife, Apollo, Euryalus* and *Juno*.

staff officers was now twice that of the academic staff and with the first graduate entrants the average age of cadets had begun to rise by a decade. Indeed, the transformation of Dartmouth since the end of the Second World War had been of a more fundamental nature than that which had occurred with the move from *Britannia* to the College and the introduction of the Selborne Scheme. But as Davies and Grove were to conclude:

> 'The College's aims, the inculcation of a broad view of the naval profession, the development of the conduct and sense of duty required of an officer and the preparation of officers for further training, remain what they always have been. They are grounded in three-quarters of a century of tradition, for change at Dartmouth is always tempered by stability.' (1980, p.24).

The Last Twenty-Five Years

The 1980s saw the continuation of the tradition of change at Dartmouth. The decade started bleakly for the Royal Navy. The previous twenty years had already witnessed the withdrawal of British forces from 'East of Suez' and the last of the true aircraft carriers, HMS *Ark Royal*, had been decommissioned in 1978 to be replaced by the smaller Invincible class carriers. Against a back drop of the economic and political decline of Britain and the deterioration of East-West relations, further defence cuts were envisaged by the defence review conducted by the newly elected Thatcher government, under Secretary of State for Defence Sir John Nott. The Nott Review of 1981 threatened to reduce the Navy to a comparatively small specialist anti-submarine force within NATO, with drastic cuts in platforms and personnel. However, the Falklands conflict of 1982 was to prove a dramatic reminder that Britain retained crucial interests outside the North Atlantic and that the Royal Navy was still required as a tool of foreign policy, to transport and supply forces across the globe, and to deploy and protect amphibious forces. The success of the campaign served to boost Britain's standing in the world and critically saved the Royal Navy from some of the more draconian measures that had been proposed, but thankfully not yet implemented, in the Nott Review. Moreover, a new generation of Dartmouth graduates had found themselves successfully tested in the theatre of war.

One of the most evident changes felt at Dartmouth, however, was a reflection of the transformation of the educational system with the introduction of comprehensive schools and the expansion of the universities from the late 1960s. The increase in the number of university graduates lead to a steady rise in average age of officers under training, so that by 1988 the average age had risen to twenty-three years and 73% of full career officers either had a degree on joining or would have obtained one by the end of their training. Thus the Navy was recruiting more graduates, but it was still those who entered straight from school that were more likely to remain in the Service and to make the Navy their chosen career. The Navy had encountered a problem of retention that had been slowly growing since the 1960s, as graduate entrants were far more likely to see the Navy as a stepping stone to another career later in life, and only sign up for a short career commission. To combat this situation the Navy considered the introduction of an in-service degree, as many school leavers were actively being encouraged to go to university before embarking upon a career.

This inevitably required the training methods at Dartmouth to be scrutinized, and the establishment of a new ethos at Dartmouth appropriate to a tertiary training establishment. Having staved off the suggestion to close the academic department completely it was decided in 1988, under Captain John Brigstocke, to introduce a new degree. This was the College's first foray into degree level work, through which Dartmouth would teach the first year and the final two years would be completed at the Royal Naval Engineering College, Manadon. Students would then be awarded the new degree of BA in Maritime Defence, Technology and Management, often referred to as the 'Dartman' degree. The Council for National Academic Awards (CNAA) awarded the final degree but it was Director of Studies Ian Jones who undertook much of the groundwork. One of the requirements of this transformation was that time be made available for the staff teaching on the degree programme to engage in subject development and research. A number of new appointments were made in the academic faculty to bring in those with research experience and a background in academic publication, in particular a new Director of Studies with a background in university teaching, Dr Alan Machin, was appointed in 1988 to demonstrate Captain Brigstocke's 'determination to signal that BRNC was into tertiary not secondary education'[8]. The degree was launched in 1990 and continued until Manadon closed in August 1995.

The overall effect was to finally cull those elements of the public school atmosphere that had continued to linger in the College since the mid-1950s. Meanwhile some of the more childish rules and activities were eliminated and 'all night leave' was finally to be granted to Young Officers. The bells signalling the changeover between periods were abandoned and in order to fit the maximum amount of material into the limited time available the fifty-five minute teaching period was reduced to forty-five minutes, although as one lecturer at the time recorded, this transition was not without its difficulties:

> 'Unfortunately, the implementation of these new arrangements coincided with the replacement of the original electro-mechanical master timing system, which required a complicated and time-consuming placing of pegs in holes in order to sound

Previous pages: Aerial view of the College in 2002.

8 Personal communication from Admiral Brigstocke.

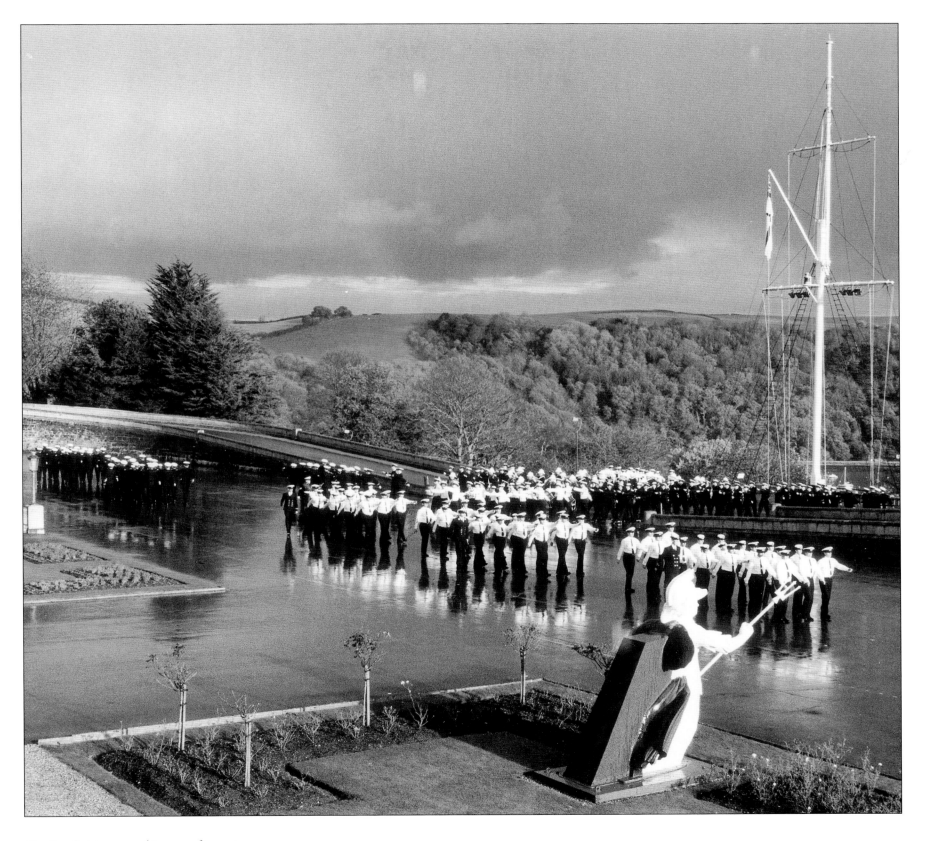

Practice divisions marching on after a storm.

Man overboard.

Essential maintenance: Top: The clock receives a face-lift.
Bottom: Stonemason works on the Royal coat of arms on the clock tower.

Cadets by example than any one else in the College. Every cadet is therefore allocated to a 'Guiding Sub Lieutenant' or 'Sea-Daddy'. They will discuss with the Cadet their general progress at regular intervals and by pointing out their faults they can make the new entry feel at ease and will almost certainly be able to contribute to the Cadet's general naval training. Every Cadet is allocated to one of five Divisions, named after a famous Admiral; Jellicoe, Blake, Hawke, Cunningham and St Vincent. Each Division is headed by a Lieutenant Commander, he supervises the Cadet's training and administrative needs and will ensure that every cadet does his bit for the Division – on the sports field, on the river or in some other useful way: always watching for signs of weakness so that early steps may be taken to reject unsuitable characters – he will go out of his way to assist a Cadet who finds some part of the course difficult to master. Each Cadet is allocated a Civilian Tutor who will assist him if he finds problems with academic training. The Tutors report on the Cadets in their 'tutor sets' – so providing a double check on the Cadet's progress. Most Tutors are permanent staff so they fulfil the valuable task of continuity, since Divisional Officers remain in the College for only two years. The most important Sub Lieutenant, as far as the new entry is concerned, is the 'Divisional Sub Lieutenant' who is chosen for his qualities of leadership and personal bearing. He is responsible for organising the Division and ensuring that the Cadets meet high standards in such matters

On 26th July 1972 The Dartmouth Training Squadron, with ships specifically dedicated to the training of cadets from BRNC, was disbanded. The DTS did continue for another twenty years but the College had to bid for sea-time for the cadets and a variety of ships were used, although the two LPD's (the Assault ships Fearless and Intrepid) were commonly in use for the purpose. However with a shrinking Navy the RN could no longer afford ships dedicated to training and the ships became dual role while under the Captain DTS. Below is a list of some of the vessels used, but a scarcity of available information means that the list is incomplete.

1973	HMS Intrepid	Assault Ship
1974	HMS Fearless	Assault Ship
1975	HMS Intrepid	Assault Ship
1976	HMS Fearless	Assault Ship
1979	HM Ships Fearless, Intrepid and Hermes	Assault Ships and Aircraft Carrier
1980	HMS Intrepid	Assault Ship
1981	HMS Londonderry	Fleet Trials Ship
1983	HM Ships Fearless and Rothesay.	Assault Ship and A/S Frigate
1984	HM Ships Plymouth, Berwick and Londonderry	Fleet Trials Ship and A/S Frigates
1985	HM Ships Fearless and Glamorgan	Assault Ship and Type 42 Destroyer
1986	HM Ships Fife and Juno	Destroyer and A/S Frigate
1987	HM Ships Bristol, Euryalus, Juno, Fife and Rothesay	Destroyer and A/S Frigates
1988	HMS Bristol	Destroyer
1989	HM Ships Bristol, Euryalus and Achilles	Destroyer and A/S Frigates
1990 – 1991	HM Ships Bristol, Ariadne and Minerva.[1]	Destroyer and A/S Frigates
1992	The Dartmouth Training Squadron was replaced by Initial Sea Training (IST) which was principally undertaken by Batch 1 Type 22 Frigates, initially led by HMS Brilliant.	

HMS *Cumberland* from an old postcard.

HMS *Isis* from an old postcard.

HMS *Euryalus* visiting Dartmouth in April 1989, flying the paying-off pennant in her final deployment. Her commanding officer was Commander J. P. Cardale who subsequently joined the College as The Commander.

HMS *Bristol* visits the College in 1991 prior to paying off. Her Captain, Richard Hastilow took up his next appointment as Captain of the College.

Cadets on board HMS *Isis* (c. 1902-1903).

1 At the start of 1991 saw the ships *Bristol, Ariadne* and *Minerva* all sailing for the Western Mediterranean to take on the primary task of patrol ships for that area after the escalation of hostilities in the Arabian Gulf. This meant that their training role, though still an important aspect of their work was to become a secondary consideration.

Cadets are expected to perform various College duties each term, as members of the Divisional Guard, as coxswain of the Duty Motor Cutter on the river, as members of the Colours and Sunset flag party or perhaps as the Commander's Messenger.[3] However trivial the duty two things are important: firstly, for many the duty will be their first taste of responsibility, with penalties to be awarded for failure; secondly, the prestige of the Division is at stake if things go wrong – very often the scorn of his fellows is the worst punishment a Cadet could suffer! Throughout the Cadets' training they are learning to carry out simple tasks correctly so that the greater responsibilities that they will have in the Fleet will be second nature to them.

To be able to relax for short periods becomes vitally important to Cadets after they have concentrated hard on their studies during the long days at Dartmouth.[4] Culturally the Britannia Society of Music and Arts, caters for most tastes by arranging regular performances by well known artists in such widely differing fields as folk music and ballet; an annual College Play that is entered for the Inter-Command Drama Competition; an annual College Revue and the provision of facilities for giving music lessons on instruments from piano to the guitar. It is very easy for Cadets to forget the world outside after the first few days within the organisation[5]. A NAAFI canteen is provided for the use of Cadets in the evening, but only beer is sold, but a television and snooker table is provided.

With the basic theoretical knowledge under his belt the Cadet is ready to put ideas into practice at the end of his second term at the College and he joins one of the three frigates of the Dartmouth Training Squadron[6]. The sole function of the Squadron is to take Cadets to sea for the whole of their third term. With the first year of training behind them the Cadets become Midshipmen and leave Dartmouth for the Fleet.'

This is the routine that both HRH The Prince of Wales and HRH The Prince Andrew would have been trained under and much of it is still recognisable by those who have passed through more recently, and as such it provides a valuable insight into the life of a junior officer under training at Dartmouth.

The smell of floor polish is one of the most evocative memories of the College.

One of the major changes at Dartmouth, which will be obvious from the account above of 1971, is that women have been for the past fifteen years an integral part of not only College life, but also of life in the Royal Navy. Another major change is that the rank of Cadet is no longer in existence, it having being abolished in 1972, when all junior officers training at the College would become Midshipmen. Although the term, not rank, Officer Cadet is still in use for those who join BRNC. In 1973 BRNC opened its doors for the training of female officers for the first time in its history, the first group being a number of QARNNS (Queen Alexandra's Royal Naval Nursing Service). This heralded the way for further training of females at the College as the WRNS officer-training course moved form Greenwich to Dartmouth in 1976 and 'Talbot' Division[7] was formed to house them. The first females to train in the all male dominated BRNC must have found life quite strange; the following account was written by Surgeon Lieutenant Susan F Good, who joined the College in 1973.[8]

3 Little has changed here except that the Duty of Commander's Messenger has disappeared. Duties with rather more responsibility are given to senior Young Officers today, such as the Assistant Duty Commanding Officer (ADCO) or Duty River Officer, the former assisting the DCO and the latter organising the river activities.

4 To this end a young officer will snatch sleep whenever he can, often on coaches going to a sports fixture and occasionally during an academic period. One of the authors (RP) remembers taking a group of young officers to RNAS Culdrose some years ago and once in the minibus all thirteen of them were asleep by the time the bus had reached the top of 'College Way'.

5 Everything that the Cadet should need is provided, such as a cobbler, tailor, hairdresser and even a cash dispenser.

6 See box relating to the DTS. Today a junior young officer will spend about six weeks on board a ship as part of his 'Initial Sea Training'(IST), this system having replaced the DTS in 1992.

7 Named after Mary Talbot, Director of WRNS 1973-76. Talbot Division lasted until January 1992 when women were totally integrated into the Royal Navy.

8 First published in the *Britannia Magazine*, Christmas 1973.

Handing over the staff of office, Commander Richard Marshall hands over to Commander David Vaughan in 2002.

Defence diplomacy: Commander-in-Chief of the Ukraine Navy Admiral Yezhel visiting the Engineering Science laboratory in November 2000.

A regular sight in recent times, a Merlin HM1 helicopter 814 Naval Air Squadron landing on the Parade Ground.

'I should imagine that the idea of a female Royal Navy Officer passing through the male dominated corridors and classrooms of The Britannia Royal Naval College would bring shudders of horror to the more traditionally minded officers. Nevertheless I had the honour to be the first – a Surgeon Lieutenant (D) in the NEO Class of 17th September to 12th October 1973.

On arrival I committed the great sacrilege of parking on the parade ground. After reporting my presence, I was escorted to my cabin by a Midshipman and helped to unload the car – advantage number one of being female. The following day I mustered for introductory talks with members of the QARNNS and with other the female new entry, Constructor Midshipman Claire. Amongst other things we were told about the swimming test. In theory this was not compulsory for Midshipman Claire and myself, but a challenge was thrown

Operation Fresco. College personnel stand in during the fire-fighters strike in 2002.

down in such a away that neither of us could really refuse. The idea came as rather a shock as I had played no games for about eight years. In fact I had little difficulty either with swimming or the treading water test (in spite of the large boiler suit). However, I could not pick a brick up from the bottom of the pool and so became a 'backward swimmer'.

Normally groups only attending the College for short periods do not do 'early morning activities' unless they are 'backward swimmers'. Then they have to report to the pool every morning at 0630 until they pass the test. I did not have to do this – just another of the very many occasions when being a girl was a definite advantage.

To avoid having to apologise for bad language and blue stories, my colleagues elected me an 'honorary gentleman', though after medical or dental school they need not have worried. It was really quite amusing in lectures for the class to be greeted by a 'good morning gentlemen' with the addition of 'Oh' I do beg your pardon, when I was noticed. Certain members of the staff persisted in calling me 'Sir' because of the gold stripes.

Dr. Alan Machin, Director of Studies, enjoying International Day in the Senior Gun Room, an opportunity for international students to display the culture of their country.

Outreach. A class from Dartmouth Primary School visit the meteorological station in 2002.

Our gym sessions proved to be the next problem. I was quite prepared to join the men for gym, in spite of my unfitness, to give everyone a good laugh at least. I did not have any kit but was assured that this could be supplied. However, for some reason the gym lessons did not materialise, though I did join the men for a session in the pool with a life raft. After it had been turned upside down, I was allowed to be the first to right it. Could this be preferential treatment? The coffee with the instructor most certainly was.

Accommodation was an interesting problem. Originally I had been allocated to Hawke Division and was supposed to share a cabin with one of the doctors. After it was realised that my name was Susan, this mistake was rectified and I was transferred to C Block with the QARNNS and Midshipman Claire. In this wing we do not appear to be subjected to 'rounds' or inspection. At meal times the stewards occasionally

Fleet Air Arm day, Lynx Mk 8 when local schools are invited to the College.

come round with second helpings and, when I caught a heavy cold, the bar stewards supplied me hot toddies to take to bed.

I have enjoyed our various excursions. During our fire fighting course at HMS *Raleigh* the nurses and I were led round the inside the smoke chamber by lads working in that department – a comfort that I am sure the men in the group neither had nor would have appreciated. We have had two days at sea – one in HMS *Undaunted* and the other in HMS *Walkerton*. On *Walkerton* I was entertained in the Wardroom whereas the men had to go to the Mess–deck. I actually succeeded in hitting the lock hard enough the first time to enable the anchor to go. I had been warned previously about having to buy a round of drinks if I missed!

Another item worthy of note is Parade Training. I had never done anything like it before. Our Parade Training Instructor was

a bit surprised to find out about me but seemed to accept me very well. I took part in the Tuesday and Thursday Divisions and also in the weekend Ceremonial Divisions. I did not double with the men, nor did I carry a sword[9], though I was allowed to practise some sword drill, which was very amusing.

The most interesting social function I attended was the Senior Gunroom Ladies Night. I think that I was probably the only member of the Mess to take a male guest!!

The final escapade on which I was somewhat spoiled was Divex (Divisional Exercise) on Dartmoor. Originally I had been told that it would be a gentle stroll across part of the moor, staying in a tent overnight. I agreed to go thinking that it would

9 The carrying of swords by female officers would not come about until their full integration into the Navy in 1992.

Visiting cadets from the Japanese National Defence Academy with Modern Languages lecturer Dr. Ian Roberts in 1998.

i.

ii.

iii.

iv.

v.

vi.

vii.

On the Moor. *i. Arrival by a Merlin Mk 3 helicopter from 28 Squadron RAF in Bosnian livery. ii. Typical Dartmoor weather. iii. Nearly there! iv. Blisters. v. Mustn't fall in! vi. Cold and wet. vii. Final debrief.*

Mess Dinners

One aspect of life in the Royal Navy is the Mess Dinner, where officers dine formally together. This may be to celebrate a special occasion such as Trafalgar Night or Taranto Night, or it may involve the 'dining out' those officers who are leaving, although the Navy does not need a special excuse to dine formally. At Dartmouth there is one combined mess dinner a year held to celebrate Trafalgar Night, where the Wardroom and Senior Gunroom messes dine together in the Senior Gunroom. The Young Officers will also have the opportunity to attend their Squadron Dinner and New Entry dining in, held after their initial training phase. At Dartmouth these dinners are regarded as training events and the young officers will receive a 'brief' prior to the dinner on etiquette and the format of the evening. They will probably be required to host a member of staff and although the event is part of

their training the aim is that it should still be an enjoyable evening as they begin to realise that they have joined a rather exclusive and prestigious 'club'.

The 'rig' for the evening will be announced beforehand, and is Mess Dress, which comprises miniature medals, a stiff shirt and white waistcoat, usually worn if Royalty or Flag Officers are being dined, but Mess Undress (soft pique shirt, with blue waistcoat and miniature ribbons) is more usual.

The format of most Mess Dinners follows a set procedure, which will only vary in slight detail. A bugle is sounded ten minutes before dinner and when ready the Senior Steward reports to the Mess President (The Commander at BRNC) who takes the Guest of Honour, and precedes the Officers, into the dining room to the sound of the band playing Roast Beef of Old England. The Chaplain, if present will, say Grace before which nothing on the

An early photograph of the dining hall, laid for a formal dinner.

A chef prepares chocolate 'ships of the line,' for a Trafalgar Night Dinner.

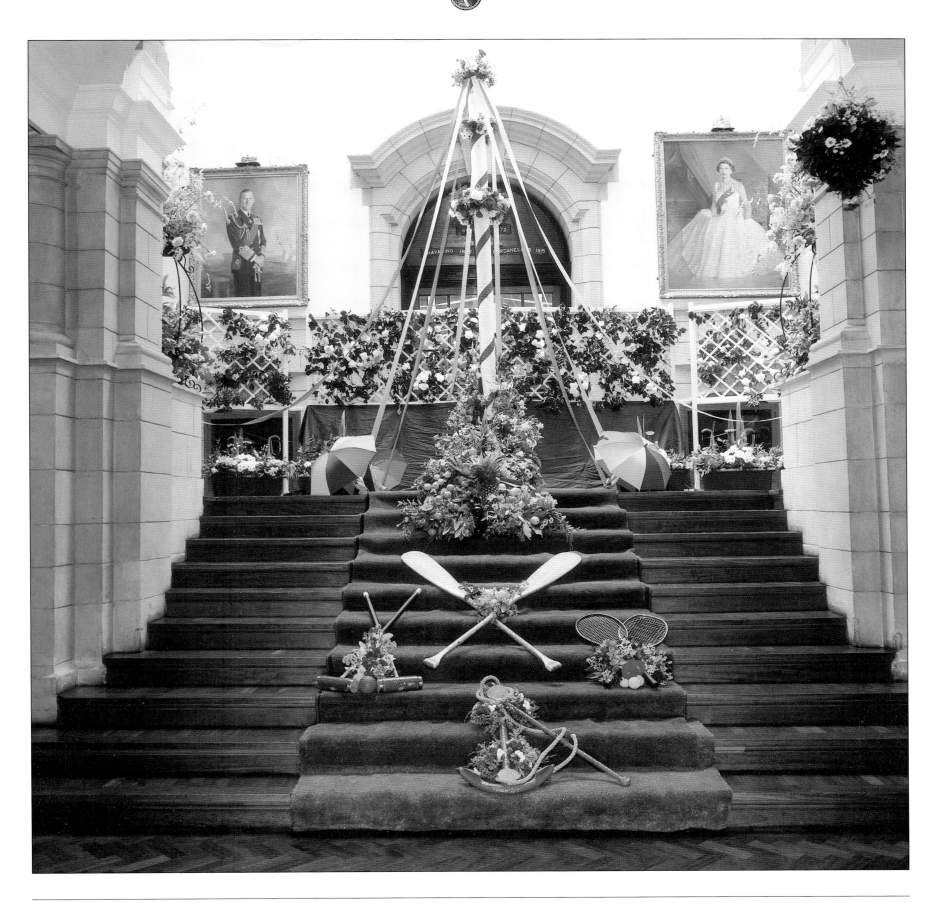

'A Young Officer in 2003'

'The rate at which time passes, as many YO's will attest, is not constant. In my initial weeks at the College each day would last an age, each PT session an aeon and three terms may well have been an eternity. But now that my training is approaching its end, the weeks slip by without being noticed and, unlikely, as it may have seemed when I was in New Entry, I almost feel as though I'll miss the place.

I may just be being sentimental, and time has almost certainly numbed the pain of all those period zeros[10], but my time here seems to be not quite so bad. It was however undoubtedly tough at times. New Entry was dominated by periods of manic haste, when it seemed that you would never be ready in time for rounds, and then battles of self-control, as it was always when you were exhausted that a lecture would be held in a warm, badly ventilated lecture theatre. A happy consequence of this part of training being so difficult was the sense of achievement after you completed it. Although few of us would have wished to spend time on Dartmoor in November where sleep and dry clothes drift into distant memory, everyone knew they had achieved something when it had finished.

The heart of the second term is the six weeks every YO spends living alongside Junior Rates at sea. At the end of this lengthy deployment the Officer Cadets return to the College as wise old men of the sea, call everyone 'shippers' and spend a lot of time brushing the salt from their shoulders. Initial Sea Training consists of a good deal of cleaning, leaning about life afloat and constantly trying not to get caught in a 'wind-up' by the Senior Rates, who revel in sending YO's to non-existent departments. This year the Lord High Admiral's Parade came at the end of my second term, so we provided the Guard of Honour for his Royal Highness, Vice Admiral The Prince of Wales.

The senior term is remarkably different from the previous two. By now it is assumed that the parade training, early mornings and lots of inspections have done their job and more emphasis is now placed on academic subjects. The senior term brought with it membership of the Senior Gunroom. As well as being able to eat in much grander surroundings, the SGR mess functions are almost legendary. The Socials Reps outdid themselves with everything from horseracing to heroes and villains fancy dress nights. The summer was also now upon us and it is difficult to resent instructing on the river in such good weather. It was not all fun and games however; the stress of constant inspections is replaced by the stress of imminent examinations. The stress level becomes apparent when lengthy conversations are heard in the SGR about whether Flight eat more than their fair share of sandwiches.

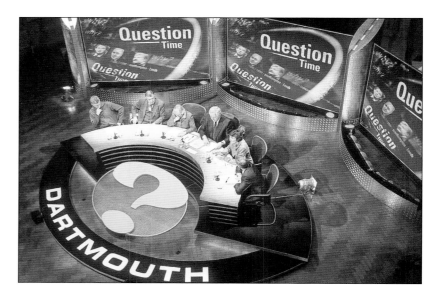

BBC Question Time on the Quarterdeck in 2003. Other television and radio programmes recorded at the College include the Antiques Road Show, Mastermind, Songs of Praise, Just a Minute and Any Questions?

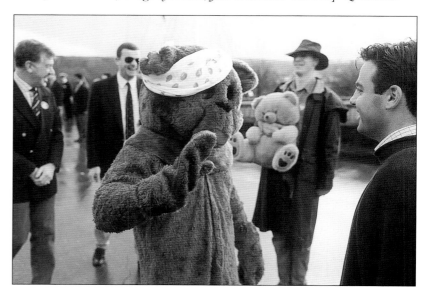

Pudsey Bear takes the salute at charity divisions for Children in Need in November 1997.

This term was the first term of the new six entry scheme, so as well as an entry at the beginning of term, there was also one half way through. As one of the legacy entries, our training was not particularly affected. All we had to do was to get to grips with what the different Phases of training equated to in the old system.

10 The period beginning at 0600, before breakfast.

Commodore Tony Johnstone-Burt 'Splices the Mainbrace' in honour of HM The Queen's Golden Jubilee in 2002.

As I write this our Passing Out Parade is just over two weeks away. The day we all thought would never arrive is just in front of us. After this we will disperse amongst the Fleet for Common Fleet Time, or go to the first stage of flying training. It will have been almost a year since we arrived through the gates on the coach from Totnes station and, for one reason or another, I expect it will be a year that none of us will forget quickly.' (*Britannia Magazine*, 2003).

Any history of the College will, as this has, relate largely to the training of Young Officers by the Naval and Academic staff but of the 350 people employed by the College, 250 of them are local residents that rely on the College for their livelihood. These are the people that keep the College running on a day-to-day basis by providing essential services such as buildings and grounds maintenance, catering, transport, cleaning services, administrative and secretarial support. Much of this work was in the past done by permanent staff employed by the College on a permanent basis, but as the world changes so do attitudes towards business. The catering was privatised in 1986 and that heralded the way forward. The cleaning services followed some time later, but the next major privatisation was that of the maintenance services at Sandquay to Vosper Thornycroft Marine Services, (VTMS). Today the commercial partner, 'Flagship Training Ltd'[11] an organisation founded in 1996, supplies much of the Service Provision. In 1996 'Flagship Training Ltd' signed a fifteen-year agreement with the Ministry of Defence to enter into a unique partnering arrangement with the Royal Navy's Recruiting and Training Agency (NRTA), and in doing so ushered in a new era in naval, industrial and management training. One of the aims of the agreement was to increase training opportunities for non-Royal Navy students within the Royal Navy training organisation. Flagship markets Royal Navy training expertise and courses to overseas navies, related naval markets and to UK industry as a whole. Royal Navy or 'Flagship' personnel working to the highest standards set by the Royal Navy deliver any training purchased through 'Flagship'. Every aspect of training, from course design to delivery is subject to an internationally proven quality control system which has been in use and continually refined in all Royal Naval training establishments for many years. The commercial partner provides two main pillars of support for the College, firstly and perhaps the most important, is the 'service provision' whereby it has taken over and now runs most of the essential services mentioned above, although today much of the general maintenance and grounds work is contracted out, and secondly to provide an income generation potential by utilising any spare capacity that the College may have.

As Britannia Royal Naval College enters its second century much has changed to affect its daily life; the age of cadets, the shifting emphasis from academic to professional training, the total inclusion of women, the application of technology and the contracting out of essential support services. The previous one hundred years have proved that without the ability to change and reflect society Dartmouth could not have survived as a Naval College. However, while the means have continually changed over the past century there remains continuity in the aims and objectives of the College: to maintain the highest qualities of command, leadership, intellectual development and humility, which combine to produce an Officer of the Royal Navy. Although composed fifty years ago, John Masefield's words still resonate[12]:

> In all the waters that are Britain's walls
> The seamen face the issue as it falls
> Against all Death that shatters and appals.
>
> Often the issue is at touch and go
> Between a few ships and a foreign foe,
> How close the issue only seamen know.
>
> Through fifty years of strain and overstrain
> Within these precincts men have come to train
> That Right may stand, that Britain may remain.
>
> Well have they struggled both in peace and war,
> Through grimmer tests than aught prepare them for,
> To keep the Seven Seas and hold the shore.
>
> Long may such Courage guard, such Wisdom guide
> The men who sail all seas on every tide
> To save the Queen,
> That she may prosper, and Her realm abide.

11 Flagship Training is a Vosper Thornycroft joint venture company, (in collaboration with BAE Systems).

12 This poem penned by the Poet Laureate for the fiftieth anniversary of the College, appears in the *Britannia Magazine* for July 1955.

Into our Second Century

On arriving to take command of BRNC prior to the College Centenary year, I was apprised of a Destroyer captain's exploits during the Second World War. He had an arduous war, much of it spent off Norway, with officers and crew largely comprising those with hostilities-only and Reservist backgrounds. When asked what kept him going he replied that more than anything else, he was not prepared to let his Dartmouth term-mates down. I hope and believe that such ethos and spirit remains the key factor in the training and preparation of the young leaders who pass through the gates of BRNC today, as they have for one hundred years (with the exception of a short break due to enemy action). Whilst retaining this fighting spirit, the young people who study at Dartmouth have changed markedly over the period. Not least, the young twelve to thirteen year-old schoolboys have become mature women and men with an average age in excess of twenty-three on entry, who now come from a wide variety of nations and creeds and bring a remarkable breadth of academic backgrounds. It is a testament to the brilliance of Aston Webb's original design that the College remains fit for task, with real estate largely unchanged except for additional accommodation required prior to the First World War. Set this against our life at sea; as recorded in this book the College grew from wooden-walled ships moored in the Dart. It now serves a Fleet where undreamed technologies then, such as missiles, nuclear power and aviation, are now established facets of our daily business. In the current dangerous and unstable world that pitches young officers into operational theatres often straight after they finish training and requires them to lead in complex environments like the Gulf, the need for training of the highest calibre remains fundamental, and the relevance of what we do here has never been more clear. People – their calibre, motivation and competence remain the most important component of operational success. Within these buildings BRNC continues to develop fighting leaders in a manner that ensures its future as the centre of excellence for leadership. The broadening acceptance of BRNC's primacy in leadership training is resulting in industry choosing to exploit opportunities here, and I anticipate closer links with Exeter University's Leadership Centre. The calibre of both our current officer cadets and staff provides exciting options for the future of the College. Links with Plymouth and Exeter Universities are developing to provide undergraduate, post-graduate and research opportunities.

Dr Jane Harrold and Dr Richard Porter have researched BRNC diligently and well. They have managed to capture the history and development of our College in lively and readable prose that serves to mark the Centenary in a most appropriate way, recording the evolution of Royal Navy officers who, when called on, fight and win. Their work detailing how this has been achieved over a century during which conflict has been a regular feature will be of interest to all who have passed through the College or to those who have an interest in naval history.

Commodore R.J. Ibbotson DSC Royal Navy
Commodore BRNC

The Britannia Association

If you are a graduate of the College, a current Wardroom member of the staff, or an officer (serving or retired) in the Naval and Royal Marines services who joined through another route, you are now eligible to join the Britannia Association. The Association is a charity formed to promote military efficiency by maintaining contacts between past and serving officers, fostering their *esprit de corps*, comradeship and welfare and preserving College traditions. It is unique amongst other naval and military associations in providing a focus from the Royal Naval College, Dartmouth.

His Royal Highness, The Prince of Wales, provided the impetus for the Association's formation in 2001, believing that the College should become a real and meaningful point of convergence for all those who have been connected with its history and training provision during their lives. The Navy, unlike the Army, does not have regimental associations, which help keep officers in touch with one another. To date, the Britannia Association has received over £600,000 in donations, gift-aid subscriptions and legacies. It has already provided two Cornish pilot gigs for the College and a third is currently under construction. These gigs are very popular amongst the cadets, who take them all over the country for competitive sport. Their achievements in the 2004 World Championships demonstrate an ongoing commitment to keeping this seafaring tradition alive.

Other Association contributions to enhancing College life include the provision of some beautiful works of art, currently on display in the main passageway in front of the College, and refurbishment of the Britannia Association Common Room. The latter provides a home and first stop for BA members, as well as a peaceful, spacious area for academics and other College staff to use in their busy working lives. The Association has also refurbished East Gate Lodge, a property available for members to rent at a very reasonable price when they wish to stay in Dartmouth.

Kevin Pyne

BRNC Cornish pilot gigs Leander *and* Bacchante *at the Isles of Scilly World Championships in 2004.*

The website (www.britanniaassociation.org.uk) is now established and is steadily growing in the amount of information and services provided. Key to this is a chance for members to locate old friends and to network on a business level. The website is also supplemented by regular production of a glossy bulletin, sent out widely amongst the Fleet as well as to all BA members.

The Association is also responsible for carving a special place in the naval history books. In April 2004 it organised (by kind permission of the Lord High Admiral) a dinner in Buckingham Palace for all serving and retired officers of Flag Rank and General Officers of the Royal Marines. With some 255 attendees on the night, such a prestigious gathering had never been held before.

BA members have a membership card, which allows them access to the College and many of its facilities. In these times of tightened security, members are asked just to let the Main Gate (on 01803 677244) know a little in advance of their proposed visit. Members may moor their boats on a buoy off Sandquay at a discounted cost of £5.00 per day (again, some prior notice to the River Officer on 01803 677088 is appreciated).

Members who want to catch up with fellow alumni in the surroundings of their *alma mater*, can use the College for reunion dinners and cocktail parties. Again, prices are now subsidised for members and the cost per head depends upon the choice of menu and wines selected. Anyone who wants to avail themselves of this facility should contact the Hotel Services Manager on 01803 677117.

The business of the Britannia Association is managed by its Honorary Secretary/Treasurer, Commander Charles Howeson RN (Rtd). He can be contacted on 07000 000 007. Also, Louise Hardy (2/0 WRNS Rtd) provides a focus within the College on a part-time basis and is always happy to answer queries from members. She can be contacted on her mobile, 077368 13476.

George Bodnar

Commanding Officers of BRNC, past and present, with HRH The Prince of Wales at the Britannia Association Dinner in Buckingham Palace, April 2004.

Back row, left to right: Rear Admiral Robin Shiffner CB, Commodore Philip Masterton-Smith Royal Navy, Captain David Bailey Royal Navy, Rear Admiral Roy Clare, Rear Admiral Mark Kerr, Captain George Tullis CBE Royal Navy, Commodore Richard Ibbotson DSC Royal Navy, Captain Richard Hastilow CBE Royal Navy, Commodore Tony Johnstone-Burt OBE ADC Royal Navy

Front row, left to right: Admiral Sir John Brigstocke KCB, Vice Admiral Sir John Forbes KCB, Admiral Sir Gordon Tait KCB DSC, Vice Admiral HRH The Prince of Wales KG KT OM GCB, Admiral Sir David Williams GCB DL, Vice Admiral Sir John Martin KCB DSC, Admiral Sir Nicholas Hunt GCB LVO DL, Rear Admiral Sir Paul Greening GCVO

APPENDIX I

Chronology

1843	The term 'Naval Cadet' used officially for the first time, though the term had been in common use for many years previously.
1857	Admiralty decides officer cadets should serve on board a training vessel, initially HMS *Illustrious* at Haslar Creek Portsmouth.
1859 1st January	*Illustrious* replaced by HMS *Britannia*.
1860	HMS *Prince of Wales* launched (later HMS *Britannia*)
1863 30th September	*Britannia* arrives in the Dart.
1864	HMS *Hindostan* arrives.
1869	Second *Britannia* arrives in the Dart (previously HMS *Prince of Wales*)
1874	Committee set up and chaired by Ad. E. B. Rice to look into health and general training of cadets.
1875	Rice Committee reports that a college should be built on shore.
1876 July	Committee under chairmanship of Ad. G. G. Wellesley formed to look into the acquisition of a site and considers thirty two sites.
1877	Prince Albert Victor and Prince George (later King George V) join as cadets.
1878	Passing Out photographs first taken.
1878	First Beagle pack founded.
1884 February	*Britannia Magazine* first published.
1884 May	The *Wave* arrives, (barque rigged vessel of 300 tons)
1885	Yet another committee suggests moving training to The Solent.
1895 15th November	Admiralty Board proposes to revise existing cadet training scheme.
1896 March	First Lord of the Admiralty announces that a new college will be built at Dartmouth.
1900 18th April	Admiralty accepts tender from Higgs & Hill to build the college for £220,600 in three and a half years.
1902 7th March	Edward VII lays the Foundation Stone.
1902 September	Sick Quarters opened, three years ahead of the main College.
1902 25th December	'Selborne Memorandum' on officer training published.
1903	Cyril Ashford appointed as first Headmaster of RNC Osborne.
1903 September	RNC Osborne opens. Introduction of the Selborne Scheme.
1903	Prof. J A Ewing appointed as Director of Naval Education from University of Cambridge.
1904	Battleship HMS *Britannia* laid down and the old ship became known as HMS *Britannia* (hulk).
1905 14th September	College opens.
1906	Swimming bath opened.
1906	Masters' Hostel opened.
1906	Rifle range under arches in use.
1907	First introduction of the new six term scheme. (Blake, Drake, Grenville, Hawke, Rodney (later re-named Exmouth) and St Vincent.
1907	E Block opens.
1907	Swimming bath covered in.
1909 May	Prince of Wales (later King Edward VIII) joins as an 'Exmouth' term cadet.
1910	New squash courts completed.

Acknowledgements

Anthony Aylmer, Rev John Beadle RN, Lieutenant John Beattie RN (Rtd.), Laura Barlee, Lieutenant Niall Benfell RN, Gary Bodinnar, Lieutenant Tim Boughton RN, Admiral Sir John Brigstocke KCB, Rev Alison Britchfield RN, Rev Kenneth Bromage RN, CPO Nick Carter, Commander M G Chichester RN (Rtd.), Don Collinson, Quintin Colville, Jan Cowling, Dr Harry Dickinson, Sir John Drinkwater QC, Brian Edgington, Lieutenant Commander Carlos Edwards MBE, Michael Floyd, David Gallop, Margo Garcia Almo, Philip Grove, Louise Hardy, Margaret Harrold, Michael Hill, William Hodges, Adrian Holloway, Michael Hunter, Rachael Johnstone-Burt, Colin Keating, Joslin Landell-Mills, Lieutenant F Mauron FN, Lieutenant Gareth Mawdsley RN, Rev David McLean RN, Brian Parker, Karen Peach, Dr Duncan Priestly, Fred Radcliffe, Carol Rampling, Dr Paul Rampling, Dr Ian Roberts, Lieutenant Commander M Rix GN, Rev Peter Scott OBE RM, William Searle, Rear Admiral Robin Shiffner CB, Gillian Smith, Anne Tasker, Gordan Thomas, Martin Thomas, William Thomson, Robert Veale, Robert Wardle, Lieutenant Omar Wheatly USN, Admiral Sir David Williams GCB DL, Captain David Wixon RN (Rtd), Michael Zollo and the staff of the Dartmouth Museum and Cookworthy Museum, Kingsbridge.

Special thanks to Keith Franks for taking and printing many of the photographs, Mandy Shepherd for the cover painting and other drawings in the book, Richard Kennell for his assistance in the library and historic book collection, Michael Pearce for supplying much valuable material, Mark Grove for sharing his historical knowledge, Rear Admiral Roy Clare for his valuable assistance and guidance, Commodore Tony Johnstone-Burt RN and Commodore Richard Ibboston DSC RN for their contributions, Rear Admiral Mark Kerr, Commander Richard Marshall RN, Commander Max Rance RN, Commander David Vaughan RN and our families and colleagues at BRNC for their support during the project.

We have made every effort to ascertain the copyright of material used in this book but where we have not had success or used material inadvertently, please could the copyright holder contact us so that full credit can be given in the next edition.

Dr Jane Harrold and Dr Richard Porter